T0158996

Influences of the Will

START DIRECTING YOUR WILL TO CREATE THE GOD DESIGNED DESTINY FOR YOUR LIFE

HERMON T. COTTON

authorHOUSE®

AuthorHouse™
1663 Liberty Drive
Bloomington, IN 47403
www.authorhouse.com
Phone: 1 (800) 839-8640

Published by AuthorHouse 07/02/2019

ISBN: 978-1-5462-5950-3 (sc)
ISBN: 978-1-5462-5949-7 (hc)
ISBN: 978-1-5462-5948-0 (e)

Library of Congress Control Number: 2018910686

Print information available on the last page.

This book is printed on acid-free paper.

TABLE OF CONTENTS

ACKNOWLEDGMENTS

I vaguely remember one of the saddest days of my childhood. I was ten years old when I got the news that my sister had passed. I remember running outside and sitting in the ditch in front of my house crying because of the anger and array of emotional influences that came over me. I didn't know how to handle it, but I knew my life would be forever changed because of her missing presence. That day it really dawned on me that she was ill. Being the youngest of eight siblings, I simply tried to just stay out of the way of everybody having the right to whip me. So before that day, I did not realize the toll that cancer had taken on my sister because she lived so full of life. Her will to live outshined all the negative attributes that came with cancer. When I look back on our life, we never treated her like she was handicapped, and she never allowed us to treat her as if she needed us to live her best life. It was almost like she took cancer by the throat and said, "Hold on because the roller-coaster ride is still moving."

Before being diagnosed with cancer, she decided to run track and field for our local high school (Humphreys County High School). She was so excited to be running track with her friends and classmates. At the team physical, they drew blood and the doctor noticed something was not right with her blood. He requested that my mom take her to UMC Hospital in Jackson, Mississippi. Then UMC referred her to St. Jude's hospital in Memphis, Tennessee. That was the day we found out she had bone cancer (osteosarcoma). My oldest sister, Deborah, recalled having a conversation with her on that day. Brenda said, "They said I've got cancer, but I don't feel that sick. I don't have cancer." Deborah looked at her and said, "Really? Cancer? You are going to be fine."

So Brenda kept living her life to the fullest in spite of her illness. There were times when her ankles would swell, and she would say her legs felt hot or painful, but she never stopped moving even after the doctor had to amputate one of her legs. After being told that she had six months to live, she fought cancer back for an additional blessed ten years and seven months. She refused to be put in a box. I can remember her being the only fearless girl on the block with one leg to ride our homemade go-cart. She did all my sisters' and neighbors' hair, loved fashion, played kickball, graduated from high school, enrolled in college, and loved to travel and meet new friends. Most of all she taught us what it meant to be a part of a family. Family members should always be willing to support one another, especially when uncontrolled circumstances cause life to be challenging. She also taught us how to inspire one another and be inspired. Although we are far from perfect, we all know the beauty of family supporting family through challenges.

Brenda and our family could not have weathered the storms of cancer without the help and support of extended family, friends, neighbors, and church family. They all played a vital role in supporting and encouraging us day in and day out. To this day we all stay in touch with Brenda's friend Craig Irwin because of his unfailing friendship that my sister valued so much. The Dodd family provided a home away from home where she could go when she wanted to simply get out the house. Reverend Dodd actually gave Brenda a room in the house, although we lived right across the street. Also countless neighbors, cousins, and friends kept her playful and spirits lifted. A special thanks to Mrs. Gertude Clemon and Uncle Po (Alonzo Young), for constantly being supportive of our family and making sure she had a memorable summer vacation in Detroit, Michigan.

So in remembrance and acknowledgment of Brenda Faye Cotton's will to live and pursue life, I am encouraged and inspired to be willing to live my best life now.

PREFACE

Why God Is After Your Will

God created the humans with the intention of having them represent His authority on the planet He had created.

—Dr. Myles Munroe

Foundational Scripture: *Mark 8:34 (KJV): "Whosoever will come!"*

It's been said that the will is the most powerful and awesome gift God has given to humankind. It allows us to decide to act against our creator or act in alignment with the will of our creator, God almighty. Humankind was created to produce glory that will last throughout eternity. The will is defined as expressing the future tense, inevitable events, a request, or facts about ability or capacity. However, I define the will as a God-given tool with the power to influence your actions and restrain you according to your God-given purpose in life. The will is meant to be an agent or tool of our identities that allows God's will to be executed on earth once we align our will with His. The power of humankind's will allow us to control our impulses, actions, and directions of destiny and apply self-control.

We were created to be thinking beings, capable of making rational decisions and rapid judgment calls in alignment with God's Word. We are adept at visualizing abstract concepts, designing complex machinery, and developing

The Will Is the Tool That God Placed in Humankind's Image and Likeness

Influence of the Will #1

God loves you just the way you are, but he refuses to leave you that way. He wants you to be just like Jesus.

—Max Lucado

Foundational Scripture: *Genesis 1:26a (KJV): "And God said, 'Let us make man in our image, after our likeness.'"*

Animals live and survive on instincts. Although we humans have instincts that are beneficial to our lives, it is our will and mind that sets us apart from other species. When I was a young boy, I had a dog that was not a house dog. During the winter, I wanted to bring him in the house, but my parents would not let me. I can still see my dog sitting by the front door, trying to absorb whatever warmth he could coming from underneath that door to stay warm enough to survive. His instincts are what placed him there.

Likewise, everyone in our family stayed around the heater in the house to keep warm based on our instincts and need to survive. It was humankind's will that created the heater for the house. All year round, both humankind and animals find ways to adapt to the environment. If dogs had the will to create a heater to use in the winter, they would, but they don't. We have to provide the heater for them.

"And God said, 'Let us make man in our image, after our likeness.'" Being made in God's image and likeness automatically puts us into a place of dominion for the purpose of managing and cultivating the environment we reside in. This is why God immediately announces our role of having dominion over all that creeps on the ground. By identifying what to have dominion over, God clarifies what is not in humankind's dominion. God never said we could have dominion over other humans, but society has taken the influence of resources and used them to persuade the actions of other humans to make them subject to their conditional environment. There is no other god to tell almighty God what He should do with His creation. This is why God clarifies Himself as God alone. Isaiah 45:5 (KJV) says, "I am the Lord, and there is none else, there is no God beside me: I girded thee, though thou hast not known me." Creation is made from purpose, and the creator owns the purpose of the creation. Therefore, when God decided to place His image and likeness in humankind, He gave us the tool of the will so we could create glory in the earth.

Our will comes from the identity of our creator. It cannot be controlled by another because the character of the will requires self-control. Nothing controls God or His will. God's will is His Word, and no external influence can manipulate it. Matthew 24:35 (KJV) says, "Heaven and earth shall pass away, but my words shall not pass away." This is why slavery has never been of God and therefore could not continue. No one can control the human will; it is a gift from God to be used for His glory.

Since God creates nothing without purpose, what then is the purpose of the human will? Because we are created in God's image and likeness, our will is also a reflection of God's will. God's will created humanity for His glory. Ephesians 1:9–12 (KJV) says:

> Having made known unto us the mystery of his will, according to his good pleasure which he hath purposed in himself: That in the dispensation of the fullness of times he might gather together in one all things in Christ, both which are in heaven, and which are on earth; even in him: In whom also we have obtained an inheritance, being predestinated according to the purpose of him who worketh all things after the counsel of his own will: That

> we should be to the praise of his glory, who first trusted in Christ.

The purpose of our will, therefore, is to manifest God's glory on earth. When we are able to create, do, and be an expression of God's Word on earth, we are properly using our will for God's glory.

Thoughtful Moment

Scripture: Philippians 2:5–7 (NKJV): "Let this mind be in you which was also in Christ Jesus, who, being in the form of God, did not consider it robbery to be equal with God, but made Himself of no reputation, taking the form of a bondservant, and coming in the likeness of men."

Conceptual Principle: The will is the tool God placed in humankind's image and likeness that gives us the ability, by faith, to express God's glory.

Question: How does God's image and likeness express itself in your life?

Notes

The Will's Influence on Planning

INFLUENCE OF THE WILL #2

We often can't see what God is doing in our lives, but God sees the whole picture and His plan for us clearly.

—Tony Dungy

Foundational Scripture: *Hebrews 11:1: "Now faith is the substance of things hoped for, the evidence of things not seen."*

No one plans for something undesirable for themselves. Once our desires and purposes are clear, we should be willing to plan. Planning is one of the most recognizable forms of faith. When we believe and have faith in God's word, it allows us to walk in faith and manifest the plans God has placed in our heart. This allows God's will to manifest something from the spiritual realm in the natural realm through our faith. Our willingness to plan aligns us with the truth of God's Word, which makes God's resources available.

A great example of the will's influence on planning is a blueprint. A blueprint of a building about to be constructed outlines the cement, foundation, electrical wiring, plumbing, voltage capacity, and type of flooring needed. All this planning and more is required before one nail is hammered. Someone had to be willing to research all that information. Someone initiated their will to pursue each of these areas to create a desired vision of a building.

While the designer is stretching out the blueprint on paper, there are no resources or materials. They are simply drawing out of their vision and the existing materials that they are aware of. The designer is turning thoughts that are made of words into a completed picture with as many details as possible. In the designer's mind, all the resources are there, so they have the freedom of unlimited creativity at their fingertips. If the designer needs a million gold bricks, they can draw a million gold bricks. A designer creates with purpose and functionality, so if they only need one hundred thousand gold bricks to create the building they desire, they don't draw a pile of nine hundred thousand gold bricks in the blueprint. So being willing to plan requires you to have purpose and functionality in mind, just like God had your purpose and functionality in mind when He created you.

One must examine every aspect of a plan before instituting it. The first step of God's will for us started when He created humans by breathing life into Adam. God's blueprint started with the plan of salvation for humankind after the fall. It began with the birth of Jesus Christ, His death on the cross, and His resurrection. Though we make many plans, they are not always in the will of God. Our plans tend to fall by the wayside because we base them on whatever circumstances are happening in life or what we would like to happen in our lives. When we place our faith in God, He steps in. Once we acknowledge Him, He then begins to direct our paths according to Proverbs 3:5–6: "Trust in the Lord with all thine heart; and lean not unto thine own understanding. In all thy ways acknowledge him, and he shall direct thy paths." God's will for us continues to evolve on a daily basis. Jeremiah 29:11 (NIV): "For I know the plans I have for you," declares the Lord, "plans to prosper you and not to harm you, plans to give you hope and a future." Since He already has plans for us, then let us place our plans in God's hand for direct alignment.

Thoughtful Moment

Scripture: Proverbs 16:2–4 (NIV): "All a person's ways seem pure to them, but motives are weighed by the Lord. Commit to the Lord whatever you do, and he will establish your plans. The Lord works out everything to its proper end even the wicked for a day of disaster."

Conceptual Principle: Planning clarifies our vision. Our vision aims at our goals or purpose. Our purpose shapes our desires. Our desires influence our will. Our will activates our ability to plan; therefore, we are able to see the end from the beginning.

Question: How does your planning help validate your faith in God?

Question: How does God's image and likeness express itself in your life?

Notes

Destiny Moments Created by the Will

Influence of the Will #3

You never know when your life is about to change. You never know when one decision will dramatically impact your life and change the course of your destiny.

—Dani Johnson

Foundation Scripture: *Proverbs 3:5–6 (KJV): "Trust in the Lord with all thine heart; and lean not unto thine own understanding. In all thy ways acknowledge him, and he shall direct thy paths."*

Our will is being engaged twenty-four hours a day. Our next decision can be the one that places us in alignment with our destiny. When I started writing this book, I was curious about only one topic: free will. This topic opened my life to the destiny path I am on today, and I am sure it will influence a future moment of destiny that I have yet to encounter.

The engagement of the will is like a waterfall that consistently falls on a rock. After a period of time, the impact dents the rock where the water has been falling and becomes visible. Each drop of water represents one decision we make during any given day. Our will to make a left turn at one intersection will lead us to the next intersection of our lives, which will automatically lead us to our destiny. Mike Murdock said, "Success is made up of a series of constant accomplishments." But our failures help shape the path to our destiny just as our accomplishments do.

President Nelson Mandela of South Africa had the will and passion to fight apartheid and spent more than twenty years in prison for doing so. He must have felt like a huge failure every day he spent in prison, waking up to prison bars staring him in the face and living in an environment created for criminals. I am sure there were moments when he thought he had failed to reach his destiny.

But at the moment he realized he was the destiny, his will became aligned with the purpose God had created for him. Far too often, we focus more on what God puts around us than what God puts in us. When we realize we are the freedom, deliverer, overcomer, and more than a conqueror, we become settled in our being. At that point, our impact becomes so automatic that we don't have to turn it on or off because it's always on.

I love watching President Mandela's interviews. He is so poised. His words are authentic, his emotions are balanced, and he stays focused on his destiny no matter what questions the interviewer asks. Each day he spent in prison obviously taught him how to focus on his purpose and be willing to pursue it with unwavering faith to see it come to pass. So decide today to possess your daily dominion and cultivate your life purpose with intentional daily actions.

Thoughtful Moment

Scripture: Proverbs 3:5–6 (KJV): "Trust in the Lord with all thine heart; and lean not unto thine own understanding. In all thy ways acknowledge him, and he shall direct thy paths."

Conceptual Principle: The human will is being engaged constantly. With each decision and initiation of the will, we are shaping our destinies for either God's glory or our own human desires.

Question: How do the daily decisions of your will create your destiny?

Notes

The Will in Relationship to Persistence

INFLUENCE OF THE WILL #4

God knows our situation; He will not judge us as if we had no difficulties to overcome. What matters is the sincerity and perseverance of our will to overcome them.

—C. S. Lewis

Foundational Scripture: *James 1:4 (NKJV): "But let patience have its perfect work, that you may be perfect and complete, lacking nothing."*

The Parable of the Persistent Widow

> Then Jesus told his disciples a parable to show them that they should always pray and not give up. He said: "In a certain town there was a judge who neither feared God nor cared what people thought. And there was a widow in that town who kept coming to him with the plea, 'Grant me justice against my adversary.' "For some time he refused. But finally he said to himself, 'Even though I don't fear God or care what people think, yet because this widow keeps bothering me, I will see that she gets justice, so that she won't eventually come and attack me!" And the Lord said, "Listen to what the unjust judge says. And will not God bring about justice for his chosen ones, who cry out to him day and night? Will he keep putting them off? I tell you, he will see that they get justice, and quickly. However, when the Son of Man comes, will he find faith on the earth?" (Luke 18:1–8 (NIV)

Be persistent by executing your will in one area and then spreading it to other areas. This allows you to start in one place and finish where God calls you to be. If we understand the will, it has no choice but to submit to us because we know God's original purpose for it. The will was designed to create glory to God in the earth.

Persistence is the ability to pursue something's original purpose. So we have to know what that original purpose is in order to be persistent. The character of persistence is steadfast and established in truth to the point of purification or restoration to meet its original design and functionality. God is so specific about His creation design and functionality that He made it persistent in its genetic makeup. For an example, if you take a seed and let it dry out for months or years and then take that same seed and put it back in the ground, the persistent genetic traits will cause germination and birth the fruit or tree. We are not so different; there are countless stories of individuals who received Jesus Christ as their Lord and Savior and now their lives are so fruitful.

Your persistence in faith can move mountains both physically and spiritually. The will of persistence allows us to fix our faith in God because we understand the original purpose and intent. Once we understand God's purpose for something, our faith becomes fixed because we see it the way God sees it.

Faith is our belief in what God said in His Word. When we believe God's Word, we allow our will to express persistence, which then gives us the ability to stand on God's Word. When our understanding is aligned with God's, we understand that what we are persisting in must bend and lend itself to our God-given command. Therefore, it's not that you are in control of God's creation, but you are commanding it to do the purpose and function God created it for.

Thoughtful Moment

Scripture: Galatians 6:9 (KJV): "And let us not be weary in well doing: for in due season we shall reap, if we faint not."

Conceptual Principle: Once decided, the character of the will transforms into persistence, which creates a tenacious will to pursue either God's glory or our human desires.

Question: How does the principles of your faith support your will to be persistent?

Notes

The Will to Simply Try Again or Start Over

INFLUENCE OF THE WILL #5

God never promises to remove us from our struggles. He does promise, however, to change the way we look at them.

—Max Lucado

Foundational Scripture: *Isaiah 43:18–19 (NIV): "Forget the former things; do not dwell on the past. See, I am doing a new thing! Now it springs up; do you not perceive it? I am making a way in the wilderness and streams in the wasteland."*

We have to try different things before we are mature enough to make correct decisions. We have all failed at something: parenting, career, losing weight, budgeting, relationships, and so on. Seldom do we marry the first person we date; we usually have to date several individuals to discover what we really want in a mate or understand what we should not want in a lifelong partner. Most important, even as believers, we fail to obey God at all times. So the will to try again affects all our lives at some point in time.

Many things cause people not to try again, but we don't have that option. One of the first things we have to overcome is the failure of the last attempt. That failure can sometimes appear as rejection, disappointment, and even depression. Sometimes we fail because of our own perception of the goal we are pursuing.

In trying again, we also have to overcome a lack of support from other people. This causes us not to believe in ourselves. Every day we are granted new grace and mercy to live the abundant life despite the challenges we face.

Many people are recovering from different types of addictions: drug addictions, sexual addictions, behavioral addictions, social addictions, and so on. I knew a man who struggled with drug addiction. Even though he always told others that one day he would be free from his addiction, those he associated with, including family and friends, didn't believe it. Some treated him as if he had no right to be free. They even laughed at him when he declared his freedom from addiction.

He carried around a little notebook where he had written the dates on which he had tried to stop his addiction. He wrote on his tenth attempt that he didn't do drugs for eight hours. On his fiftieth attempt, he went without drugs for two days. On the seventy-eighth attempt, he went without drugs for four days. On the ninetieth attempt, he went without drugs for seven days. On his one hundredth attempt, he went without drugs for two weeks. After that, however, he relapsed when his brother died tragically.

But he had one addicted friend who always supported him. He told him that every day he did not do drugs he had a reason to live. So on the one hundred eighteenth attempt, he used the inspiration of his friend to mark every day for him not to do drugs. On his twenty-fourth day of not doing drugs, he finally realized he had broken his addiction. It was like the freedom he finally experienced gave him the motivation to go and do unimaginable things in life. He added one success story after another because he never stop pursuing his goals.

Having the will to try again is vital to God maturing us for His glory. God understands that we don't have it all together and that we don't know everything, but our faith in Him is the gift of life that allows us to keep pressing toward the mark for the prize of the high calling of God in Christ Jesus. This is why He grants us new grace daily and His grace abounds much more where sin abounds. Because of Jesus Christ, the grace of God is ever flowing toward us. So even if we find ourselves on the edge of life one day, like the man on the cross with Christ, we can try again and be received into the kingdom of heaven.

Thoughtful Moment

Scripture: Psalm 145:14 (NIV): "God upholds all who fall The Lord upholds all who fall and lifts up all who are bowed down."

Conceptual Principle: Losing the will to try again can destroy our future destiny and God's glory for our lives. There are many reasons for being unwilling to try again, but they all result in not manifesting our purpose and destiny for our lives. God is constantly doing new things with each generation, so trying again is simply maturing and being transformed by His Word.

Question: What is the one thing you believe God wants you to try again?

Notes

The Will to Believe God for Healing

Influence of the Will #6

The man who is going through with God to be used in healing must be a man of long-suffering.

—Smith Wigglesworth

Foundational Scripture: *Hebrews 11:6 (KJV): "But without faith it is impossible to please him: for he that cometh to God must believe that he is, and that he is a rewarder of them that diligently seek him."*

When I was a child, I had asthma so bad my mother used to make pillows for me from the moss off the trees to help me breathe. My father, being a minister, constantly prayed for me to be healed and anointed my head with oil. My parents' efforts helped me become healthier.

By the time I was ten years old, however, I was tired of suffering from asthma. It had become such a nuisance. But because I saw it that way, I began to lose sight of the efforts my mother and father were making. I began to accept that if it was time for me to die, it would be okay because it was better than living with asthma. Little did I know that all I went through was leading me to the place in God that would birth my healing! I began to believe God, not just for healing but for a life in Him.

When I accepted Jesus as my Lord and Savior, I understood that God was the head of my life. That belief changed my life so I could receive the healing my body needed. The will to believe in God to be God regardless of the need gives us access to healing. God has already provided healing through His precious Son, Jesus Christ. Isaiah 53:5 says, "With his stripes we are healed." The stripes Jesus endured bear witness to Him being God's willing authority to heal.

Our will to believe in Jesus gives us access to the life God designed, which includes healing. Jesus healed people before He went to the cross. Luke 17:19 says, "Your faith has made you well." How was Jesus able to heal before the cross? He would ask people if they believed. The scriptures tell us stories of people who came from great distances to see Jesus because of their will to believe Him. In Mark 5:25–34 (KJV), it says:

> And a certain woman, which had an issue of blood twelve years, and has suffered many things of many physicians, and had spent all that she had, and was nothing bettered, but rather grew worse, When she had heard of Jesus, came in the press behind, and touched his garment. For she said, If I may touch but his clothes, I shall be whole. And straightway the fountain of her blood was dried up; and she felt in her body that she was healed of that plague. And Jesus, immediately knowing in himself that virtue had gone out of him, turned him about in the press, and said, Who touched my clothes? And his disciples said unto him, Thou seest the multitude thronging thee, and sayest thou, Who touched me? And he looked round about to see her that had done this thing. But the woman fearing and trembling, knowing what was done in her, came and fell down before him, and told him all the truth. And he said unto her, Daughter, thy faith hath made thee whole; go in peace, and be whole of thy plague.

It is our faith in God that allows His healing, favor, and blessing to flow into our lives. Like the father of faith, Abraham, even our righteousness is commuted onto us by faith. The Bible said Abraham believed in God and connected to Jesus Christ's grace and righteousness through faith. If you can have faith and believe Jesus Christ is the Son of God, our resurrected Savior, and the healer for the world, His healing is yours to receive. You have every right to healing; just like salvation, it's a part of the Jesus Christ salvation package. He doesn't come in pieces; He is our total blessing, secure hope, and only complete plan for salvation and eternal life.

Thoughtful Moment

Scripture: John 6:29 (KJV): "Jesus answered and said unto them, this is the work of God, that ye believe on him whom he hath sent."

Conceptual Principle: The will to believe in God gives us access to all of God's promises through and in Christ Jesus. Healing is a promise for the redemptive price Jesus Christ paid on the cross. First believing in God almighty allows the healing authority of Jesus Christ to be made available to you.

Question: Do you believe in Jesus Christ as your Lord, Savior, and healer?

Notes

You Are the Will of God Almighty

Influence of the Will #7

We are not built for ourselves, but for God. Not for service for God, but for God.

—Oswald Chambers

Foundational Scripture: *John 1:4-5 (KJV): "In him was life, and that life was the light of all mankind. The light shines in the darkness, and the darkness has not overcome it."*

What God wants He wills it to be. The Bible says God's Word will not return to Him void; rather, it will accomplish the thing it has been sent to do. God's desires are written all over us in our gifts, talents, purpose, and destiny. He has already sent His Word to create our being. We are here because God spoke us into existence according to His will. We are sons and daughters of God because we come from Him. That's why we cry out "Abba Father" and "creator of all things." Most parents see their own features and characteristics in their children. It's the same with God; He is mindful of our divine characteristics.

We are not on this earth by accident. The true and living God almighty had a will and a desire for us to be here. He formed us in our mothers' wombs for His divine, holy, life-fulfilling destiny and purpose. We are one of a kind, never to be duplicated, never to be repeated or reproduced at any time in the past, present, or future. It does not matter if some relatives have the same features or mannerisms; there is always some difference, even in twins. We are all the world will ever get, our mold has been broken, and our God-essence will fulfill its promise and purpose for His glory. We begin to experience God's glory (presence and goodness) at the moment of accepting Him as our Lord and Savior. We are carrying around the glory of God in the life we breathe daily. All of heaven and earth are awaiting the glory we are created to birth and share with the world. Our energy and spirit are eternal and everlasting in Christ Jesus.

We have not evolved from monkeys because monkeys need something else to become the animals that they are. When I go to the zoo, I see that the monkeys are still there and they are happy to be monkeys. God did not create humankind to fulfill the purpose of a monkey; He has called us into being to express His glory as we fulfill our God-given purpose. If God wanted animals to create heaven on earth, they would be building houses, highways, the internet, skyscrapers, airplanes, rockets, and the list goes on. God made us for all the wonderful, awesome, and miraculous creations that exist.

God almighty's will for us is to serve Him by serving and encouraging others. "God is not unjust; he will not forget your work and the love you have shown him as you have helped his people and continue to help them" (Hebrews 6:10 NIV). "But exhort one another every day, as long as it is called 'today,' that none of you may be hardened by the deceitfulness of sin (Hebrews 3:13 ESV). One of Jesus's attributes was to be a servant, not to be served. We are a part of God's will. We are here on earth and celebrating life and enjoying family, friends, and other associates. I often listen for the unnamed peoples that played vital roles in the lives of individuals whose names are world renounced. Then I want to say thanks to them because their words of comfort or wisdom that were given at the right time were truly pricelessly. I think about all the civil rights members and freedom riders who were listed and those that were not listed on record. I think of the countless number of slaves who gave life itself to birth us into today, and their courage and sense of divine justice is just as glorifying to God as the latest million-dollar invention or technology advancement. We are all connected in God our Father and in life as brother and sister through life many generations.

Thoughtful Moment

Scripture: Matthew 28:19–20 (NLT): "Therefore, go and make disciples of all the nations, baptizing them in the name of the Father and the Son and the Holy Spirit. Teach these new disciples to obey all the commands I have given you. And be sure of this: I am with you always, even to the end of the age."

Conceptual Principle: We do not exist because of our own will; it is because of God's will that we exist. The Bible and all creation clearly tells us we are not made of ourselves but of God's will. The creation always comes from the Creator. Inasmuch, we are made in God's image and likeness for His purpose and not our own. We exist for His purpose and not because we evolved into existence.

Question: Do you believe God wanted you to express His will in the earth?

Notes

Blind to Your Will

Influence of the Will #8

If you build your whole life on a certain idea and it becomes theory and then philosophy and then doctrine and then a belief system and finally a way of life and a mentality, you will not know that you have basically built your life on a lie.

—Dr. Myles Munroe

Foundational Scripture: *Ephesians 1:18 (NIV): "I pray that the eyes of your heart may be enlightened in order that you may know the hope to which he has called you, the riches of his glorious inheritance in his holy people."*

A concept is a thought or idea that has conceived into a mental picture. The thought of not owning responsibility for our will prevents us from owning the authority God place in us. We must acknowledge the will is a vital part of human beings, created in the image and likeness of God. The world has no God-given authority over the human will. Our will aligned with God's will gives us purpose and active dominion in the world. Jesus Christ says it best: "Nevertheless not my will, but thine, be done" (Luke 22:42 KJV). Jesus understood that God gave purpose before He gave life. This gives us a reason to explore God's will before we set off to do what feels good. One of the reasons we have turned a blind eye to the will is we don't want to acknowledge how much we all like feeling good. We'd rather promote what feels good than our God-given purpose for living by aligning our will with God's. I don't believe the cross felt good to Jesus, but it was necessary for humanity's salvation. Likewise, adults don't like to give their kids a whipping but understand when a child must be disciplined. We have become incredibly blind to managing our will in order to avoid the undeniable responsibility of managing our will.

It's as if we have been conditioned to believe we are not responsible for managing our own will. Somehow we have been so trained and sedated toward directing the alignment of our will that it has become a norm. At the same time we are constantly aligning our will to the advertisements and marketing strategies of the world. For example, now it is common to spend one hundred dollars on a pair of shoes, but also rare to give one hundred dollars in a church offering. The world is very aware of your dominion over your will. This is why companies can spend millions of dollars on commercials and marketing to engage your will constantly. For example, a commercial during the Super Bowl, which runs for less than seven minutes, costs millions of dollars to air. If it cost millions to air the commercial, then someone is profiting millions on the response of your will to that commercial.

The world has tried to blind our will by blinding our hearts. It has done this by influencing our wicked desires and then promoting those wicked desires to the world as okay and good for all. This is why Jesus tells us to guard our hearts and the gates of our souls, which give entry to the heart. The world's marketing and advertisements appealing to our wicked hearts' desires are nonstop and without filter. But I declare the Almighty is just as willing through His love to retrieve and keep those who are lost in the world. It's up to the authorized dominion keepers to align their will with God's will and pursue the world the way Christ did daily.

The world engages the will of people of every age, gender, race, religion, and social class 24-7 because Satan has no limits on who he wants to influence to sin and keep as far away from salvation as possible. To defeat the fold, Satan is advertising he's got good products to offer but knows all his products are fake. But why let worldly influences be the assessment of what God's Kingdom citizens are willing to do for and with God's people? God put His image and likeness on humankind, so He will forever be the designate assessor of His creation, not the world. "For this reason we also, since the day we heard it, do not cease to pray for you, and to ask that you may be filled with the knowledge of His will in all wisdom and spiritual understanding: that you may walk worthy of the Lord, fully pleasing him, being fruitful in every good work and increasing in the knowledge of God: strengthened with all might, according to His glorious power, for all patience and longsuffering with joy; giving thanks to the Father who has qualified us to be partakers of the inheritance of the saints in the light" (Colossians 1:9-12 NIV). The salvation of Jesus Christ is the best product or service that ever hit the world market. It's also the most reliable contract or service plan anyone can have. Lastly, it is non-discriminating to any ethnic group, sex, age, culture, or religion. As believers we must be willing to do the good work that we are created to do for the glory of God.

Thoughtful Moment

Scripture: Matthew 6:22 (NIV): "The eye is the lamp of the body. If your eyes are healthy, your whole body will be full of light."

Conceptual Principle: Nothing is done consistently without activating the will. The will is so powerful that we are afraid of misusing it because of the responsibility that comes with it. So when we act as if we are unaware of the variables that influence our will, we shift blame and responsibility to external stimuli. The world's systems take advantage of this reality by marketing to our will constantly for the benefit of their profit margins.

Question: What aspects of your will are you not considering that impact your life?

Notes

The Will to Do Wrong or Right

Influence of the Will #9

> But when the cross is working deeply a believer comes to know himself. He realizes how undependable are his ideas, feelings and desires.
>
> —Watchman Nee

Foundational Scripture: *1 Peter 3:17 (NIV): "For it is better, if it is God's will, to suffer for doing good than for doing evil."*

When I was a child, I lived with my grandmother and my mother. My grandmother showed me all the love and devotion a child could desire. She believed in God, but for some reason she would not go to church. My mother, on the other hand, went to church every time the door opened because she had been through some circumstances that grew her faith. My mother and I did not have an easy relationship, but I knew she loved me just as much as my grandmother did. It just seemed at times that Granny's love felt more like God's love.

There came a time when I began living with my mother and going to church regularly. It was then that I began to hear the Word and became aware of the Holy Spirit firsthand. Therefore, I made a conscious decision to believe in God for myself, and not because Granny or Mother believed in God. Some who know my family situation may think that Granny's love for me was right regardless of how often she attended church. Others may say my mother was wrong to let the circumstances of her life cause a separation in our relationship where I was not assured of her love.

It's amazing how we can decide whether something is right or wrong without knowing the total picture. Instead we should be thankful that

God can see all of life and still provide a Savior for us. That being said, I am happy to say my relationship with my mother is better than it has ever been and is growing stronger every day. I'm happy to say that my granny now goes to church often.

What drove me to God was the will to pursue a better relationship with my mother regardless of the past circumstances. What drew my mother to God was the will to change her life circumstances so she could have a healthy relationship with me. Granny, on the other hand, had a will to forgive people for misrepresenting God's love when she was first introduced to the church community. All of us had to manage our will to grow healthy relationships.

The will is a vital component in deciding to do right or wrong. The will is actually neutral before we make that choice. Too often we focus on our actions more than our decision to act. While some actions are primitive, most of our decisions require some level of thinking. Having said that, I would like to look at the will's engagement prior to its actions. Actions speak louder than words, but words mentally perceived produce the actions that speak the loudest.

Words are considered expressions of thoughts. John 6:63 (KJV) says, "It is the spirit that quickeneth; the flesh profiteth nothing: the words that I speak unto you, they are spirit, and they are life." Words that engage our will include desires, love, lust, revenge, forgiveness, hatred, kindness, compassion, cruelty, and the list goes on. Each of these words has an emotional expression that describes how we feel about the proposals of right or wrong that our will is engaged with on a daily basis. Our emotions toward right or wrong decisions are generally based on our experiences, reasoning, or influences, whether internal or external.

So let Jesus Christ's example on the cross help guide our decision. Christ said He endured the cross because of the exceeding weight of glory He saw after fulfilling the mission on the cross. He did not see our wrongs or our filthy righteousness; He saw fulfilling His purpose, glorifying God, and providing salvation for the world. Jesus Christ's love paid for every sin we will ever commit. Therefore the question is not about right or wrong; it is about maturing in God's will and living a purposeful life. At no time does God want his children to stray further away from his love. If Jesus asks us to forgive our brother seventy times seven, how much more do you think God can forgive us?

Thoughtful Moment

Scripture: 1 Peter 3:17 (NIV): "For it is better, if it is God's will, to suffer for doing good than for doing evil."

Conceptual Principle: The will is not biased when it comes to its functionality. The conditioning of the will is like creating a habit. The more we use it for good or evil, the more willing it is to participate in whatever we choose. Becoming aware of the variables that influence our will allows us to have the dominion God gave us as His children. No one outside of God is influencing His will. So understanding the variables of our will allows us to condition it for God's glory.

Question: Do you believe God has given you the authority over your will and grace to stay in His love?

Notes

THE WILL OF COMPASSION EXECUTED IN KINDNESS

INFLUENCE OF THE WILL #10

His is a loving, tender hand, full of sympathy and compassion.

—Dwight L. Moody

Foundational Scripture: *Luke 6:35–36 (KJV): "But love ye your enemies, and do good, and lend, hoping for nothing again; and your reward shall be great, and ye shall be the children of the highest: for he is kind unto the unthankful and to the evil. Be ye therefore merciful, as your Father also is merciful."*

Jesus Christ illustrated the precious gift of kindness by going to the cross for the sins of the world. That one act of kindness will be forever etched into humankind's existence. His will to show compassion through that one act of kindness showed how relatable He was to pain, afflictions, and suffering. Compassion comes from the root word *com-*, which means "to be with," and *passion*, which means to share the pain and suffering of another without the other person's authority to do so. Jesus not only shared our suffering and affliction of sin, but He also dismissed the aftereffects of condemnation by justifying the guilty verdict of sin's origin. "For as in Adam all die, even so in Christ shall all be made alive" (1 Corinthians 15:22 KJV).

The will to allow compassion to flow in our lives connects us to one another in both the physical and the spiritual. Seeing people in other countries dying because of the lack of food and housing connects us to their pain and suffering. When we see animal cruelty, the signs of stress and pain touch our emotions and affect our spiritual beings. Compassion allows our spiritual beings to act with kindness. It is a vital component that lets us live and exist together in harmony. It allows me to see the you that exists in me. "And Jesus, when he came out, saw much people, and was moved with compassion toward them, because they were as sheep not having a shepherd: and he began to teach them many things" (Mark 6:34 KJV).

Kindness is one of the greatest tools that believers have in the body of Christ. It is one of the most undeniable acts that presents the character of God to humanity. Everyone I have ever known who has been shown kindness has been affected in a profound way. When kindness is demonstrated, it shows the love factor in compassion. Kindness steps into our pain and affliction with us, without expectation of reward or gain. It allows the release of the oppression and conflict that is disrupting God's original intent and plan for our lives.

Compassion motivates people to go out of their way to help the physical, spiritual, or emotional hurts and pains of another. It is often regarded as having an emotional aspect to it, though when based on cerebral notions such as fairness, justice, and interdependence, it may be considered rational in nature and its application understood as an activity based on sound judgment. There is also an aspect of compassion that has a quantitative dimension, often given a property of "depth," "vigor," or "passion." The word *compassion* is from Latin, and it means "co-suffering." More involved than empathy, compassion commonly gives rise to an active desire to alleviate another's suffering. With all the components of kindness, one of its greatest is to show compassion to those suffering without reciprocating cause.

Thoughtful Moment

Scripture: 2 Corinthians 1:3–4 (NIV): "Praise be to the God and Father of our Lord Jesus Christ, the Father of compassion and the God of all comfort, who comforts us in all our troubles, so that we can comfort those in any trouble with the comfort we ourselves receive from God."

Conceptual Principle: The will to be kind and compassionate allows humankind to express the nature and character of God's love for His children. Kindness is so effective that once it is expressed, it cannot be denied because of its gift of unselfish, abounding, and freely given help or support.

Question: When was the last time you showed someone compassion through kindness?

Notes

God's Will Expressed in Jesus, the Model for Expressing Our Will

Influence of the Will #11

God will become visible as God's image is reborn in you.

—St. Bernard of Clairvaux

Foundational Scripture: *Isaiah 43:18–19 (NIV): "Forget the former things; do not dwell on the past. See, I am doing a new thing! Now it springs up; do you not perceive it? I am making a way in the wilderness and streams in the wasteland."*

God wanted humankind to understand clearly what His will looks like in humanity, so He sent His Son, Jesus, to model His will on earth. The Bible shows us three dimensions of the expressions of God. God the Creator and Father of all existence. Jesus Christ: the expression of God's Spirit in the flesh. The Holy Spirit: the government, guidance counselor, and confident source of all knowledge, abiding in humankind. In like image, God created people as a three-dimensional expression of Himself: the mind of a human is the creative reflection of the purpose of God's will. The body of a human is the chosen vessel for the capacity of the spiritual essence and physical identity of His presence. Finally, a person's soul is their will—the emotions and spiritual expression of the person. The uniqueness and similarities of both humankind and God furnishes proof that our identity was established from our Creator God. We express God through ministries, culture, art, and love. There are three types of love that we express (*agape*, or unconditional "God" love; *storge*, or empathy bond; and *philia*, or friend bond). However, we express a fourth type with our spouses (*eros*, or erotic bond). God has commanded us to love according to John 13:34–3. Showing love to one another allow others to see that we are His disciples; in other words, we are modeling after His attributes.

God's will for our lives is not a mystery that has not been revealed. Ephesians 1:9–11 (KJV) says:

> Having made known unto us the mystery of his will, according to his good pleasure which he hath purposed in himself: That in the dispensation of the fullness of times he might gather together in one all things in Christ, both which are in heaven, and which are on earth; even in him: In whom also we have obtained an inheritance, being predestinated according to the purpose of him who worketh all things after the counsel of his own will.

The Bible is a display of God's will toward humanity. It tells us God's desires for us. 3 John 2 (KJV) says, "Beloved, I wish above all things that thou mayest prosper and be in health, even as thy soul prospereth." It gives us a model of how God wants us to use our will in alignment with His. There is no guesswork involved when it comes to God's love for us and His will toward us. It also allows us to see ourselves in His image and likeness to share the bountiful love He wants us to have for one another. When Jesus Christ fulfilled the law, He was walking out God's will. So when we say we want to be more Christlike, all we have to do is find our purpose in Christ Jesus and begin walking it out by allowing the Holy Spirit to lead and guide us.

Thoughtful Moment

Scripture: Isaiah 43:18–19 (NIV): "Forget the former things; do not dwell on the past. See, I am doing a new thing! Now it springs up; do you not perceive it? I am making a way in the wilderness and streams in the wasteland."

Conceptual Principle: God wanted humankind to understand clearly what His will looks like in humanity, so He sent His Son, Jesus, to model His will on earth.

Question: How has your faith in Jesus Christ allowed you to model God's will in your life?

Notes

The Will to Forgive Seventy Times Seven (490) Times

Influence of the Will #12

And you know, when you've experienced grace and you feel like you've been forgiven, you're a lot more forgiving of other people. You're a lot more gracious to others.

—Rick Warren

Foundational Scripture: *Matthew 18:21–22 (NASB): "Then Peter came and said to Him, 'Lord, how often shall my brother sin against me and I forgive him? Up to seven times?' Jesus said to him, "I do not say to you, up to seven times, but up to seventy times seven.'"*

Finding freedom from our pain and hurt to forgive can be easier said than done. If we don't have the courage to forgive people who have hurt us, their offenses will continue to haunt us and cause bitterness to settle in our hearts. When considering forgiveness, I often think of what it took for God to forgive humankind for all the wrongdoing, hurt, pain, and evil works we have done, are doing, and will do. Jesus Christ had to really love God and understand what it meant for God to have His broken relationship with His sons and daughters mended.

Nothing destroys relationships like unforgiveness. Unforgiveness causes loved ones to stop speaking, agreeing, loving, and caring. Most of all, it tries to kill any possibility of a future relationship. Everything we do is built around relationships with others. Even God requires two or three to agree before He appears in our midst: "Again, truly I tell you that if two of you on earth agree about anything they ask for, it will be done for them by my Father in heaven. For where two or three gather in my name, there am I with them" (Matthew 18: 19-20 NIV).

Jesus Christ was telling Peter not only to forgive but also to understand that forgiveness is a characteristic of God, so to be in God we must make forgiveness part of our character. God is the ultimate example of forgiveness by loving a world that despised, hated, and did all manner of evil against Him, yet He forgave all of us.

Forgiveness is the only way to restore a broken relationship. The world itself hangs on the thread of forgiveness because we are constantly maturing and developing in areas that will require forgiveness. All of us will do something wrong that will require someone else to forgive us. God knew this so well that He placed the responsibility of salvation on the principle of forgiveness—first forgiveness from God, and then forgiveness from each other. Without forgiveness, every person we think is saved would be lost and separated from God.

This is why the will to forgive must be viewed from God's perspective and not from a trading of goods perspective. I often think of how bad of a deal it was for God to send Jesus Christ to the cross for what I did. It makes no sense, no kind of way, from the ground up, but when we understand what God has invested into humankind, it begins to make sense.

God put His image, likeness, and Spirit in us. So allowing a broken relationship to be destroyed would be like suffering daily from an illness that we already have a cure for. God loves the you that is in Himself, which is the reason He is constantly pursuing us, whether we have backslidden, lost faith, decided not to believe, killed, lied, stolen, and a whole lot more.

This is why the will to forgive is so vital to you, to me, and to the body of Christ—the church. So if we obey God's call to forgive others as He forgives us, we can be free of any painful situations, sufferings, abuse, disappointment, and bitterness and be filled with everlasting love, compassion, joy, and kindness.

Thoughtful Moment

Scripture: Ephesians 4:32 (NASB): "Be kind to one another, tender-hearted, forgiving each other, just as God in Christ also has forgiven you."

Conceptual Principle: Forgiveness is one of the most vital components of our existence. We could not live on earth together without being willing to forgive one another. We have all done something that we needed forgiveness for. So forgiveness is not only needed but necessary, like the air we breathe. This is why Jesus asks us to do so much, so that we understand its principle instead of its symptoms.

Question: How has Jesus Christ's forgiveness impacted your life?

Notes

God's Will Is His Word, His Desires, His Laws, His Principles, and Most Important, His Love

INFLUENCE OF THE WILL #13

The things you do for yourself are gone when you are gone, but the things you do for others remain as your legacy.

—Kalu Ndukwe Kalu

Foundational Scripture: *Isaiah 43:18–19 (NIV): "Forget the former things; do not dwell on the past. See, I am doing a new thing! Now it springs up; do you not perceive it? I am making a way in the wilderness and streams in the wasteland."*

Isn't it funny how the very presence of a child brings about so much without anyone saying a word? One of my children once asked me, "Mom, why are you just looking at me?" I smiled and responded, "It is amazing." She responded, "Who? Me?" And I replied, "Yes, you." When I look at my children, I don't immediately think of my efforts. I think, *Wow, the Creator has to be smart as all outdoors. How can He create a being who then creates another magnificent being? God in all His awesomeness.*

When I looked at my daughter that day, I saw personality, attributes, character, and physical features from me, her father, and her grandfather. She acts as if she likes a certain color fabric like her aunt and seems to be choosing her career path. She's also named after her maternal grandmother. As a mother, I can hardly take much credit for her successes or who she's growing up to be. It is obvious that the Creator has His hand on her life because I invited Him to keep and cover her and her brother many years ago.

When I look at my son, I'm in motion because he's a mover, and I seem to be playing catch-up. The most powerful thing a parent can do is control the environment in which their child learns and grows. Everything a parent allows in that environment will either positively or negatively affect the child's life. As the saying goes, "You teach what you know, but you produce who you are." Every example is either a positive or negative example, and many parents, including myself, want to know how to produce children with a Christlike character. So the challenge is to develop a Christlike character within yourself.

God's will is His Word; His desires; His laws; His principles; and most important, His love. The many promises outlined in God's Word are for each of us. The working of the Word guarantees us those promises and outlines the consequences for disobedience. As children grow and develop, they see this in their lives and the lives of those around them. The picture is not always pretty because sometimes triumph isn't part of the story until much later in life. The process, however, does introduce children to faith, trust, compassion, and forgiveness.

I was once watching my son play ball as I was sitting on the bleachers with my daughter. She asked me, "Mom, when am I going to find what I'm really good at?"

I told her, "In life, there are seasons and cycles. You may not feel that this is your season, but believe me, yours will come." Sometimes God requires us to celebrate someone else's season before we celebrate our own.

Proverbs 22:6 urges us to train a child in the way they should go, and when they are old, they will not depart from it. I am thankful for this scripture because it is a scripture of faith. My children don't always reflect what I am teaching, but I don't stop teaching. God doesn't always tell us, as His children, that we are doing the right thing, but He advises us to seek Him daily for direction and trust that all things will work for the good of those who are called according to his purpose.

Training a child never ends; modeling Christlike behavior for them continues throughout life. God's will is His way, which is expressed in

His Word, and the Holy Spirit within teaches us how to apply God's Word, His will. It is good to know that neither we nor our children are left alone as we journey through life. We need not fear whether we are living out God's will. We must simply invite Him daily into our lives, the lives of our children, and the lives of all those we love. We must put forth our best effort and trust that the Creator doesn't just create, He also develops, matures, and supplies provisions for His creation, which we can see all around us.

Proactive people don't just make something; they maintain it. Proactive parents produce children and provide for them. As a result, they model for their children how the Creator cares for His own.

Thoughtful Moment

Scripture: Ephesians 4:29 (NLT): "Don't use foul or abusive language. Let everything you say be good and helpful, so that your words will be an encouragement to those who hear them."

Conceptual Principle: God's will is His Word that expresses His desires, His laws, His principles, and His love the same way we express good desires, laws, principles, promises, and love to our children throughout life's journey.

Question: How does the will of your word shape and support your faith and destiny?

Notes

The Will to Be Open to New Opportunities

Influence of the Will #14

Every problem is a character-building opportunity, and the more difficult it is, the greater the potential for building spiritual muscle and moral fiber.

—Rick Warren

Foundational Scripture: *1 Corinthians 16:9 (ESV): "For a wide door for effective service has opened to me, and there are many adversaries."*

Let's consider what it takes for a fisherman to catch fish each day he or she goes out to sea. Before the fisherman even sets out, they must have the proper licenses, clothing, tools, bait, food, and water. The fisherman then has to get up early in the morning, prepare the poles, nets, and fishing line. Next, the fisherman has to travel to the fishing location and prepare the fishing spot.

Even after all this prep work, the fisherman still never knows what he or she will catch (the size or type of fish) until a fish bites the line and the fisherman brings it out of the water. Nevertheless, they are constantly open to the new opportunities of their catch for the day.

While there are countless stories of people's lives being changed, none of those changes happened without those people being open to new opportunities. God provides us with the life, the physical and mental capacity, the ability to communicate, the forgiveness, and the list goes on, so we can be open daily to new opportunities.

Sometimes we overlook what God has already invested in our potential and miss opportunities He repeatedly presents to us. The fisherman is willing to take many steps to prepare for fishing before even one fish bites the bait. We miss many opportunities because we're so anxious to catch the fish that we fail to appreciate the journey of fishing. A real fisherman enjoys being on the water, in solitude, baiting the line, and every other detail about the trip, so they can be open to the reward of catching the fish.

Psalm 37:4 tells us to delight ourselves in the Lord, and He will give us the desires of our hearts. Notice the first thing we need to do is delight ourselves in the Lord. In other words, we need to be happy with the God who loves us and wants to bring His purpose forward in our lives. God's purpose fulfilled in our lives will bring us joy; peace; prosperity; and most of all, fulfillment.

We need to decide to open our lives up to the opportunities, the journey, and the rewards God has already prepared for us. His plans for our lives are tailor-made. Not every day will be peaches and cream, but each day we live matures us to process and sustains the blessings God has for us. Just like the fisherman, our catch can happen any day as long as we are willing to execute our faith and get on the water every day that God grants us life.

Thoughtful Moment

Scripture: Matthew 7:8 (KJV): "For everyone that asketh receiveth; and he that seeketh findeth; and to him that knocketh it shall be opened."

Conceptual Principle: When we are not willing to pursue new opportunities, we close the door to destiny. God is constantly manifesting His glory in our lives, which takes us into some unfamiliar places at times, but it also teaches us how to allow God to be our constant in a world of uncomfortable seasons.

Question: What opportunity is waiting for you to explore?

Notes

God's Will in Others for God's Glory through You

INFLUENCE OF THE WILL #15

God allows us to experience the low points of life in order to teach us lessons that we could learn in no other way.

—C. S. Lewis

Foundational Scripture: *Matthew 5:16 (NKJV): "Let your light so shine among men that they may see your good deeds and give glory to your Father in heaven."*

The story of Joseph shows God's will working through others, from his birth all the way to Egypt. As much as I would like to tell you it is a joy to walk in God's will every step of the way, the scriptures and life have taught me otherwise.

Joseph had a dream that he saw his brothers bowing to him. The dream was so real to Joseph that he told his father and brothers. But because he was the second youngest son, his brothers felt as if he was being rude and disrespectful. So his brothers threw him into a pit on the trading route. While this was a difficult time for Joseph, he held on to his dream.

Next, Potiphar put Joseph in prison because Potiphar's wife falsely accused him. Then, while in prison, he met Pharaoh's former butler as well as his butcher. Then he was invited into Pharaoh's presence with the very gift that caused him to be exiled from his family, the gift of interpreting dreams. When your dreams conflict with other people it does not mean your destiny is misguided. There are times our dreams take us down a path of maturity and preparation, so we can manage our place of destiny.

With the pattern of the consequences of his discernment of dreams, most would have advised him to simply keep quiet, but Joseph had finally made it to the moment of destiny where God's will was leading him. He was finally in the presence of Pharaoh, king of Egypt, where Joseph's and other believers' lives would forever be changed. After discerning Pharaoh's dreams and saving Egypt from the famine, Joseph became second in command of Egypt.

We often talk about Joseph being blessed with the wealth of Egypt and the favor of Pharaoh as if this were the crowning moment of God's will operating in Joseph's life. But the loneliness of the pit, the deceitful day in Potiphar's house, and the humility of the prison experience were tools God used to operate His will in Joseph's life. There are times when we are on the path of destiny even though things do not look like the promises of God. In these times we need to keep our faith in the dreams God has shown us. If our destination doesn't look like the promise God gave us, it is a simply a stepping stone to place us closer to our destiny in God's glory.

God's will is sovereign. It is His Word, and His Word cannot return to Him void. Even though the Bible does not mention whether Pharaoh, Potiphar, the butler, or the butcher converted to Joseph's faith in God almighty, each of them became submissive to the anointing that was on Joseph's life. We can also look at the way Pilate and the Pharisees thought they were changing the course of God's will on Jesus's path to the cross. Little did they know that they were only bringing humanity closer to salvation.

When God's will is operating in our lives, even our enemies will act in favor of our purpose and calling. There are also times when those who are closest to us think they are harming the purpose God has for our lives when they are only positioning us closer to God's will. So being mindful of God's purpose for your life will keep you on course regardless of the mountaintops or valley experiences you may go through.

Thoughtful Moment

Scripture: Matthew 5:16 (NKJV): "Let your light so shine among men that they may see your good deeds and give glory to your Father in heaven."

Conceptual Principle: God's sovereign authority can manifest His will in and through all creation. God often allows those around us to promote His glory through us. God's plan for this glory to be expressed in our lives is so established that He is willing to use multiple resources to manifest it through us.

Question: How has God shown you favor through someone else to do a good deed?

Notes

Your Willpower to Create Glory

Influence of the Will #16

We will never be able to recognize opportunities if we first don't recognize all that we have and all that we've been given.

—Joel Osteen

Foundational Scripture: *Hebrews 10:24–25 (NASB): "And let us consider how to stimulate one another to love and good deeds, not forsaking our own assembling together, as is the habit of some, but encouraging one another; and all the more as you see the day drawing near."*

I remember the first time it became real to me that I could write a book. I was at a TD Jakes Pastor and Leadership Conference, just walking around to the vendors' tables and gathering information. Then I came close to the Sermon to Book table, and a guy named Caleb asked me about writing a book. I began to share with him an idea I had been working on for several years. He asked me how far along I was in my writing. I told him I had a lot of notes and a complete outline. After that, I began to make excuses for myself, but all the time he knew I was closer than I realized. He never let me talk myself out of writing the book.

I am so thankful that he assisted me in aligning my will with God's will to write books. It has not only blessed and inspired me, but it has inspired my entire family to know and understand that their written word matters and can be used to give God glory.

After beginning the journey and making it through the book reviews, I suddenly became aware that my will has the power to move me into the manifestation of God's glory. Now I realize that my relationship with

God is all about Jesus Christ the king and replicating His character and reproducing His will on Earth. So as believers we are constantly maturing through faith to reflect our king's culture, values, morals, nature, and lifestyle.

We often talk about willpower as if we have a choice in the matter, but I would like to discuss creating the matter for God's glory. Just like me in the previous paragraph, you may be sitting dormant with your will, waiting on a crisis, an opportunity, or a situation. Whatever the case may be, decide today to allow your God-given ideas to be released for His glory.

I was writing this book before God had completely revealed the subject matter to me. I went through several rewrites and edits, but one thing was sure: my will was aligned with God's will in doing this one thing for His glory. Now I am wide open to pursuing His glory with the idea and wisdom I have received from His Word and the Holy Spirit.

God gave us willpower to create His glory on the earth. Because the nature of the will requires self-control, it is up to us to initiate or believe God's Word to move toward His will. God's will is operating throughout the world, not just in the church. Immediately after I started writing, other God-given ideas began to manifest themselves beyond the confines of religion. God is waiting on believers to align their will with His will to create glory through technology and information.

Our willpower is designed to create maximum glory for God. It's actually coded in our nature, and it's the most beneficial life mission and purpose we can have. It also makes life worth living and brings life to us. Our will to move toward God's glory is the key to having lifelong provision and success in business, wealth, health, and relationships. There is no greater measure of success than being in alignment with God's will.

So stop sitting on that God-given idea and vision. Get up and release your willpower to create glory without limits.

Thoughtful Moment

Scripture: Galatians 5:7–9 (ESV): "You were running well. Who hindered you from obeying the truth? This persuasion is not from him who calls you. A little leaven leavens the whole lump."

Conceptual Principle: The internal and external influences around us constantly affect the decisions of our will.

Question: Does the external and internal influence of your environment promote or reject God's will for your life?

Notes

Keep Submitting Your Will to God

INFLUENCE OF THE WILL #17

Above all else, we must learn how to bring our wills into submission and obedience to the will of God, on a practical, daily, hour-by-hour basis.

—Jerry Bridges

Foundational Scripture: *Proverbs 16:3 (KJV): "Commit thy work unto the Lord and thy thoughts hall be established."*

One day my father and I were having a discussion about being a son. He asked me, "When do you stop being my son?" I pondered that question for a minute and then answered, "I think never." Then I wondered, *Do I do a sonship or be a sonship?* I then realized no one and nothing can stop me from being my daddy's son because I am his son. God sees us as His children, not as His servants that He hires and fires at a moment's notice. As most sons do, we sometimes get away from our fathers' guidance, but this does not make us any less our fathers' sons (or daughters). In fact, your mistakes give your father purpose and responsibility. As a parent who takes responsibility for my kids, I often tell them that whatever problem they have, it is a problem *we* have. I let them know that no matter what circumstance they are in, I am in it with them. God is the ultimate Father, so know that his position as a father does not change because of your disobedience. He is God and He changes not.

You, too, are no less a son or daughter of God. Once I began to understand how much my father loved me and how I could talk to him about any situation. I realized his love has enough grace to love me through my mistakes. Then I realized he is committed to telling me the truth so much that it would hurt him not to tell me what he thinks is best for me.

Now I am certain his advice is best for me even if he gives it in a way I do not understand or even if I was not listening well and failed to pick up some of the details. Or maybe I just decided to try something another way because sometimes we have to see if something works for ourselves only to find out that God's way is always best.

We walk through the God and humankind relationship to see why it is so vital to keep submitting our will to God's. John 6:37 (KJV) says, "All that the Father giveth me shall come to me; and him that cometh to me I will in no wise cast out." Our relationship with God is authentic and tailor-made to us.

Jeremiah 1:5 (KJV) says, "Before I formed thee in the belly I knew thee; and before thou camest forth out of the womb I sanctified thee, and I ordained thee a prophet unto the nations." God is so in love with the you that He made. God has enough love and grace to keep us in a position to come back to Him at any time. I am so glad God's capacity to love is not equal to humankind's and that He gives grace when needed.

God will always be guiding and maturing us in Him. By this time next year, God will have shown us another revelation about something we thought we understood or something we had no idea existed. Regularly submitting our will to God should be natural because we want to remain in a right love relationship with our Father and mature into who He created us to be. God sealed us when we decided to accept Jesus Christ as Lord and the only begotten Son of God. So when He sees us in our situations, He sees us covered with the blood of Jesus Christ, the remission for sin. It actually brings joy to God to see us coming back into a proper relationship with Him. Just like the prodigal son's father, God wants to have a feast and put on the royal robe and the royal ring of sonship and authority.

Luke 15:18–20 (KJV) says:

> I will arise and go to my father, and will say unto him, Father, I have sinned against heaven, and before thee, And am no more worthy to be called thy son: make me as one of thy hired servants. And he arose, and came to his

> father. But when he was yet a great way off, his father saw him, and had compassion, and ran, and fell on his neck, and kissed him.

Luke 15:7 (KJV) says all of heaven enjoys seeing us come back into fellowship with the Father: "I say unto you, that likewise joy shall be in heaven over one sinner that repenteth, more than over ninety and nine just persons, which need no repentance." So today make up your mind to not let any idea, person, organization, or opinion keep you from submitting your will into alignment with God's will for your life. Only you can own the life God has planned for you.

Thoughtful Moment

Scripture: Romans 8:28 (KJV): "And we know that all things work together for good to them that love God, to them who are the called according to his purpose."

Conceptual Principle: There is no end to maturing in God. To stop submitting our will to God's will is not an option. This is why God allows His grace to abound more where sin abounds. His grace is always aimed at keeping us aligned with His will.

Question: When do you use grace to bring your will back in alignment with God's will?

Notes

Your Will Affects Your Reality

Influence of the Will #18

Hope lies in dreams, in imagination, and in the courage of those who dare to make dreams into reality.

—Jonas Salk

Foundational Scripture: *Philippians 4:13 (KJV): "I can do all things through Christ which strengthened me."*

There is an old saying: "Nothing happens until it happens." The turning of our will is the key to deciding when God's will for our lives happens. Deciding in our will that we are going to allow God's will to be done opens up the resources and people God is waiting to send us to accomplish His plan for our lives. What we do with our will creates and shapes our destiny and the fulfillment of our purpose. The reality of who we truly are lies in the seat of our will. It initiates the course we decide to take and destiny we will enjoy.

The reality of our will is like going swimming. First, we have to put on the swimsuit and goggles. Then we have to put our feet in the water and eventually immerse ourselves, believing the water will keep us afloat. All these steps begin in the will. We would not put on the swimsuit and goggles and get into the water if we were not willing. In that event, the reality of us becoming swimmers would not happen.

It's like Peter on the water. As long as Peter focused and his faith was in Jesus Christ, he could walk on the water. But as soon as he took his focus and faith off the source that kept him afloat, he began to sink. Our reality also depends on our focus and faith in the source of our destiny and purpose. We have a choice to live in our purpose or continue to allow life's circumstances to push us around. I once heard a story about a set of twin guys who had an alcoholic father. Each was interviewed separately. One was asked, "Why do you drink alcohol excessively?" His response was, "My father was an alcoholic and I learned it from him." Then the other brother was asked, "Why do you despise alcohol?" He said, "My father was an alcoholic and it tore my family apart, so I hate alcohol for what it did to my father." Even though their answers were similar, one decided to set his will on making alcohol a continual part of his family, while the other decided to set his will against the source of his family's problems. Our will in relationship to our reality is no different. What we focus our will toward determines our reality. So possess your God-given identity of the will and reach your God-given purpose and destiny. It's yours, so align it with the reality of your life purpose. Aligning your will with God's will is like the unseen gravitational pull and pressure of the rain and wind, which create a path through the Earth that eventually becomes a flowing river or lake that can flow for miles and provide nutriment for many.

Thoughtful Moment

Scripture: Job 38:36 (EVS): "Who has put wisdom in the inward parts or given understanding to the mind?"

Conceptual Principle: Our will to believe and do turns our imaginations, dreams, and desires into reality.

Question: How has your will impacted your current reality?

Notes

Resting in God's Will

INFLUENCE OF THE WILL #19

> Faith is to rest, not in the best of God's servants, but in His unchanging Word.
>
> —Harry Ironside

Foundational Scripture: *Matthew 11:28–30 (NLT): "Then Jesus said, "Come to me, all of you who are weary and carry heavy burdens, and I will give you rest. Take my yoke upon you and learn from me, for I am gentle and humble in heart, and you will find rest for your souls. For my yoke is easy and my burden is light."*

Have you ever noticed how peacefully a baby sleeps? Babies don't have a care in the world. They appear to be enjoying every second of sleep. It's almost as if they are back in heaven. Even the number of times they fall asleep on any given day appears to be on autopilot. It doesn't matter where they are or what's going on around them, when it's time for them to sleep, they are out like a light.

Babies are the most vulnerable and most secure at the same time. They can't communicate words, walk, eat, read, write, drive, or see clearly, but one thing they do well is rest. We feed them, carry them, figure out what they want, and protect them with our very lives, and they can't even say "Thank you." They simply do what is natural to them: sleep, wake up for a while, eat, poop, and do it all over again. They seem to have the blueprint on resting in God's will.

On the other hand, I know adults who can't sleep for more than three hours, and then they're up all day looking for a nap. An illness, anxiety over bills or debt, or other circumstances may be keeping them awake.

Maybe they're just restless. Sleeping should be natural; we've been doing it since we were born. Whatever our reason for not sleeping, it is God's will for us to rest in Him.

Just like babies do what is natural for them to do, we adults should be doing the same thing. We should naturally gravitate to God's will for our lives. I can say from experience that unnatural habits, desires, ambitions, and promises of wealth do not lead to a peaceful life with true success. I tried pleasing people and my own selfish desires and making money the wrong way, only to realize it was the most unnatural experience I could try to keep up.

We were designed to be in alignment with God's will. That's when we're at rest in all areas of our lives. Loving God teaches us how to love and be at peace with others, even if they cause us to come out of our Garden of Eden into the wilderness every once in a while. Knowing we are walking in our God-given purpose puts everything in its proper position.

The baby knows the order of things, so he or she can stay in the bed or in someone's arms all day. Order is the environment of peace, and peace is the platform for rest. Order is not just about putting things in their place; sometimes it may be about maintaining peace in the home or on the job. There is no one way that works for all when it comes to ordering peace in our lives, but there is an order that supersedes all environmental order and that is God's presence. Jesus Christ died on the cross and sent the Holy Spirit to make sure we can stay in God's presence. Staying in God's presence assures us we can always rest in Him.

Thoughtful Moment

Scripture: Matthew 11:28–30 (NLT): "Then Jesus said, Come to me, all of you who are weary and carry heavy burdens, and I will give you rest. Take my yoke upon you and learn from me, for I am gentle and humble in heart, and you will find rest for your souls. For my yoke is easy and my burden is light.'"

Conceptual Principle: There is a rest in aligning our will to God's. This is why Jesus Christ was able to go to the cross immediately after deciding to do God's will. It is finished once the will is set in God. God's will is and has always been our designated destination and resting place. He has already prepared a place in Himself for us, so no matter how life's challenges appear to influence the variables around us, we can rest in knowing who He is and in His unlimited love for us.

Question: How does Jesus Christ's redemption allow you to rest in God's will for your life?

Notes

Your Will Is Your Own

Influence of the Will #20

Every Christian has a choice between being humble or being humbled.

—Charles Spurgeon

Foundation Scripture: *2 Timothy 2:7 (ESV): "Think over what I say, for the Lord will give you understanding in everything."*

Let's be honest. It is evident we are in control of our own will because the terrible things we hear and read in the media do not reflect God controlling our will. Even atheists are directed by their own will toward their desires. The choice not to believe in God is evidence that God does not control people's wills. Choosing not to believe in God acknowledges that God exists, but the person has decided from limited reasoning not to believe. If that person were not in control of their will, then they would not be capable of arguing for God's existence or lack thereof. Such a person would be unable to make a choice either way.

I know we often say, "God's will be done" or "If God is willing," but what do we really mean when we say these things? We also say things like, "I have free will" or "Man, I have faith in you." I believe these misconstrued concepts sedate our will. We act as if God is making us go to war, experience starvation, and commit crimes that violate one another's purpose and right to live in peace. It's sad to say, but sometimes we are even more confused by religious leaders' concept of the will because they see only what we do as a complete picture of our will, and we know that Jesus Christ's sacrifice on the cross is a perpetual payment for humankind's sin.

God cannot go back on His word. His will is His word. God has not given us dominion and then changed His mind about us. He cannot give us a will that is made in His image and likeness and requires self-control, and then take control back of that same will. Revelation 22:17 asks "whosoever will to come and take the water of life freely." *Freely* means without restriction or interference or not under the control of another——to do as one wishes. This is why you have to choose God and believe in Jesus Christ as the redemptive payment for humankind's salvation.

Your will allows you to take your thoughts out of your imagination and begin to create the reality in your life through acting on the principles and truth you believe. We only want things to the extent of our imagination and exposure; therefore, it is vital to be willing to initiate change by being willing to expose yourself to new lands. The Hebrews, for example, were delivered but not set free because of their backward thinking. So the burden of freedom is the undeniable fact of self-willing responsibilities. Your will was the only thing any slave master wanted to control, but was too foolish to realize that it was made in God's image and therefore could not be controlled. It would be out of order for anyone else to have control of your will, but the world has tricked us into thinking we are free, all the while setting traps to control whatever resources we have been given. Don't allow the world to use your will as it sees fit or until you are out of resources to give.

Thoughtful Moment

Scripture: Revelation 22:17 (KJV): "And the Spirit and the bride say, Come. And let him that heareth say, Come. And let him that is athirst come. And whosoever will, let him take the water of life freely."

Conceptual Principle: Our will is like our choice to love. We cannot make someone love us. Not even God forces us to love Him. Our will is our own because it is the nature and character of the will to choose freely.

Question: How does choosing to receive God's love impact your choosing to love another?

Notes

DAILY DIRECTION OF THE WILL

Influence of the Will #21

God's will is your deepest desires.

—Dan Brown

Foundation Scripture: *Psalm 32:8 (CJB): "I will instruct and teach you in this way that you are to go; I will give you counsel; my eyes will be watching you."*

It's amazing how an understanding of our destiny becomes clear in certain fleeting moments. Out of the blue, a flash of clarity hits us, and we realize the extent to which our will and actions have affected the world. We have seen wars tear a nation apart while at the same time bringing a group of people closer than ever. Just as well we have seen a newborn bring indescribable joy to a family, but later grow up and cause both parents and family grief through misbehavior.

This is because the daily direction of the will is subtle, yet continuous, like water dripping constantly from a faucet: gravity presses the water to drop without its permission. Yet from birth, we are taught how to direct our will by controlling how we act, speak, and respond to the pressures of life. Whether we are taught to direct our will toward good or evil, we are conditioning our will to mold our manifested desires. Our will becomes a problem when we choose to take a path that does not equal God's desired result, His will.

Often, however, Christians and non-Christians alike remain unaware of God's already existing will and its nature. There is no other god telling almighty God what to be, do, or create. He is sovereign, and no person can dictate what He should do. Because we are made in God's image and likeness, we must understand that our human will is also free by design.

This is the reason we must *will* to choose Jesus Christ as our Lord and Savior.

Let's be honest; there are times when we are tired of our self-made situations and think it would be nice if God controlled our choices. If God controlled our choices, however, we would not be acting in God's image and likeness. Revelation 22:17 says, "And whosoever will, let him take the water of life freely." We are God's children; therefore, we are the expression of His nature on earth. To express that nature on earth, we must align our will with His by choosing to accept His love. Then, like Jesus, we can naturally reflect God's will on earth.

Have you ever wondered why plants and animals exist within their natural character without being told what to do, think, or be, but humanity can *reason* what to do, think, and be or create in the world? Even the mental capacity of humanity is designed to manage the most complex systems and situations. According to US scientists, the human brain has the capacity to store 4.7 billion books—or 20 million four-drawer filing cabinets filled with text! Even people considered geniuses use only a tiny percentage of their brain capacity. It is obvious we are not meant to function as another blade of grass or a monkey. Your will was designed to make impact constantly as you engage your God-given life purpose.

Thoughtful Moment

Scripture: Proverbs 16:9 (NLT): "We can make our plans, but the Lord determines our steps."

Conceptual Principle: We have at least thirty thousand thoughts per day, many of which are not pure. This is why we must be constantly pull down every vain imagination and thought that exhausts itself against the will of God and be transformed by the renewing of our minds with God's Word.

Question: How has your will impacted your daily decisions and led you to your current place in destiny?

Notes

The Will Requires Self-Control

INFLUENCE OF THE WILL #22

If we know that the aim of the Holy Spirit is to lead man to the place of self-control, we shall not fall into passivity but shall make good progress in spiritual life. The fruit of the Spirit is self-control.

—Watchman Nee

Foundation Scripture: *Job 23:10–11 (KJV): "But he knoweth the way that I take: when he hath tried me, I shall come forth as gold. My foot hath held his steps, his way have I kept, and not declined."*

The nature of the human will fights against God's will and therefore requires self-control. Having free will means not being forced into doing or not doing something. It's the nature of the human will to be free to choose God's will; therefore, God allows nothing to stop His will from being fulfilled in our lives. God will always willingly defeats whatever is opposing His will for our lives.

For years companies have been analyzing our habits and desires to determine how to engage our wills to sell and promote their products and services. Many of these products and services are not aimed at promoting a better life or to support your wellbeing but geared directly toward their profits. Although the will by nature is free, when you been conditioned and persuaded to act on the world's suggestions, you soon forget you have a choice while following the crowd. Corporate America pays billions of dollars to figure out what it takes for you to move from your living room sofa, where you watch TV, to the mall or store to buy their products. They hire the brightest minds and best equipment to run tests on our reactions to their advertising and marketing promotions.

The world has tried to condition and cultivate our will to be swayed to constantly choose against God's will. If we honestly compare our choices with God's choices, it's obvious which choices are best for us. Our conflict, therefore, is often not knowing how to align our will to choose God's will because our will is conditioned toward worldly desires; once we align our own will with His, then God's will can direct His purpose for our lives.

First, it's important to understand we have a will to give back to God, even though it has been misdirected (potentially for many years). This involves renewing our minds—understanding and accepting the fact that our will must be given back to God. The beauty of renewing the mind to align our will with God's is a discovery, not a status.

Jesus Christ positioned us when we first accepted His love. The renewing of our minds will allow us to take the first step in becoming like the water drop—giving our will back to God. We will be so aligned with God's will that we won't push against what is naturally going to happen anyway.

It is the first step in making the impact for which God has called and purposed us.

Thoughtful Moment

Scripture: Proverbs 16:9 (NLT): "We can make our plans, but the Lord determines our steps."

Conceptual Principle: The nature of the will cannot constantly be controlled by an external force. God created us in His image and likeness; therefore, our will must be self-controlled like our Father God almighty.

Question: How does self-control impact you and how you align your will with God's will?

Notes

Reason and the Will

INFLUENCE OF THE WILL #23

Everything happens for a reason. It's all part of God's divine plan.

—Ivan Guaderrama

Foundation Scripture: *James 3:17 (KJV): "But the wisdom that is from above is first pure, then peaceable, gentle, and easy to be intreated, full of mercy and good fruits, without partiality, and without hypocrisy."*

The first tool advertising and marketing professionals use to tempt people's will is reason. They will make a person think something is perfectly good, healthy, or needed by using fancy wording, statistics, facts, or quotes. God, however, has gifted His people with reason to help sift through the world's tactics and draw godly conclusions and extrapolations from *other* information, such as that found in scripture:

> Did you know that in Hebrew the word for "darkness" is the same as the word for "ignorance"? Similarly, the word for "knowledge" in the Hebrew and Greek is the same as the word for "light". So when we talk about the world or kingdom of darkness and the world of light or Kingdom of God, we are not talking about light bulbs on or light bulbs off. We are talking about ignorance and knowledge. The prince of darkness is the prince of ignorance. He rules by your ignorance. Wherever you are ignorant, he can gain a foothold. Because of these two unseen kingdoms, we are living in a world that is always tense with ongoing territorial conflicts of interest. (Munroe 2018, 19)

In fact, God encouraged His people to reason with Him. The prophet Isaiah wrote, "Come now, let us reason together, says the LORD: though your sins are like scarlet, they shall be as white as snow; though they are red like crimson, they shall be as wool" (Isaiah 1:18 ESV). In this verse, the word for *reason* is the word *yakach* in Hebrew. *Yakach* means "to prove, decide, judge, rebuke, reprove, correct, or to judge." Thus, God was calling people to come to Him and "work out [their] salvation" (Philippians 2:12 NIV) by wrestling through difficult things to prove or decide their faith—or to be reproved, corrected, or judged.

King Solomon's reason and judgment were so profound that other kings and queens traveled great distances to seek his advice. 1 Kings 4:34 (KJV) states, "And there came of all people to hear the wisdom of Solomon, from all kings of the earth, which had heard of his wisdom." He was called to judge the case of two women claiming the same child. Through reason, he deduced what a true mother would do. He decided to tell the women to take the child and divide it in half. By reasoning, he knew the real mother would want her child to live at all costs, regardless of the situation.

As expected, the true mother spoke up to save her child's life, telling the other woman she could have the child. King Solomon drew a conclusion from that information—the one who wanted the child to live was the true mother. As a result, "All Israel heard of the judgment that the king had rendered, and they stood in awe of the king, because they perceived that the wisdom of God was in him to do justice" (1 Kings 3:28 ESV). The Holy Spirit seeks the truth and resides in believers to guide us in the ways of righteousness. God wants His people to come to Him and reason with Him about truth—His Word—and "casting down imaginations, and every high thing that exalteth itself against the knowledge of God, and bringing into captivity every thought to the obedience of Christ" (2 Corinthians 10:5 KJV).

Thoughtful Moment

Scripture: James 3:17 (KJV): "But the wisdom that is from above is first pure, then peaceable, gentle, and easy to be intreated, full of mercy and good fruits, without partiality, and without hypocrisy."

Conceptual Principle: Reason is one of the variables that influences the will. It is the power of the mind to think, understand, and form judgments by a process of logic.

Question: Have you reasoned with God's Word to strengthen your faith and align your will with God's will?

Notes

Experience Impact on the Will

Influence of the Will #24

We gain strength, and courage, and confidence by each experience in which we really stop to look fear in the face … we must do that which we think we cannot.

—Eleanor Roosevelt

Foundation Scripture: *Colossians 3:12–15 (ESV): "Put on then, as God's chosen ones, holy and beloved, compassionate hearts, kindness, humility, meekness, and patience, bearing with one another and, if one has a complaint against another, forgiving each other; as the Lord has forgiven you, so you also must forgive. And above all these put on love, which binds everything together in perfect harmony. And let the peace of Christ rule in your hearts, to which indeed you were called in one body. And be thankful."*

One facet of the will is desire, and at the root of desire are previous experiences. It's easy to look at Moses and claim he did the will of God well in his life. Moses, however, made poor choices along the way too. What was it that caused his faith to be strengthened, so he could pick himself up and do God's will after a fall?

Moses saw God's display of power as the plagues overtook Egypt and watched as God moved Pharaoh to allow the Israelites to leave. He was there when God miraculously parted the Red Sea, allowing for millions of Hebrews to cross over to freedom, and he saw the Egyptian soldiers swallowed up by the waters behind Israel. God spoke intimately with Moses on the top of Mount Sinai, and Moses likely pondered the manna God provided for forty years while the nation wandered in the desert. Moses had experienced God's power, protection, and provision. This not only transformed his mind and heart but also likely solidified his faith, resulting in alignment with God's will.

The world will try to tempt believers with internal and external experiences that mimic God's faithfulness to His children. Temporary dishonest financial gains, demoralizing relationships that appear to be fulfilling, drug and substance abuse that attempt to address physical and spiritual needs, and even religious practices and customs void of an intimate relationship with God all seem to bring satisfaction but are without meaningful life purpose. These experiences woo a person away from the desire to align with God's will.

When a person experiences God's faithfulness through trials along the journey of life, their faith is truly solidified—resulting in a will more closely aligned with God's. The outcome is a peace that surpasses all understanding, an unspeakable joy that is ever flowing, and a love that endures forever.

Thoughtful Moment

Scripture: Psalm 16:11 (EVS): "You make known to me the path of life; in your presence there is fullness of joy; at your right hand are pleasures forevermore."

Conceptual Principle: Experience is one of the variables that influence the will. Experience is the knowledge or mastery of an event or subject gained through involvement in or exposure to it.

Question: What experiences have you had with God that allow you to be more willing to align your will with God's will?

Notes

Internal and External Influences' Impact on the Will

INFLUENCE OF THE WILL #25

You never know when your life is about to change. You never know when one decision will dramatically impact your life and change the course of your destiny.

— Dani Johnson

Foundation Scripture: *Galatians 5:7–9 (ESV): "You were running well. Who hindered you from obeying the truth? This persuasion is not from him who calls you. A little leaven leavens the whole lump."*

Influences such as wealth, prolonged poverty, freedom, oppression, sickness, and health also affect a person's desire to do God's will. A person who learns he or she has cancer and may only have a certain amount of time to live, for example, often begins seeking God—even if that person has spent their life in opposition to Him. Deciding to engage God's will from the perspective of faith or fear allows you to become aware of God's sovereign power and identity. The fear of something you cannot control can cause you to misplace your faith because it only allows you to see the promises of God and not understand His purpose for your future after the fear is gone.

In the Bible, Jesus interacted with a woman who had been bleeding for seventeen years. She spent all her money on physicians and medications, attempting to find a solution to her condition, but to no avail. However, that serious health problem primed her for one short but divine interaction with her Savior—who healed her in response to her simple act of touching the hem of His garment.

Liz Curtis Higgs writes in her article "The Woman Who Touched Jesus":

> By law, her touch would have made him unclean. By grace, just the opposite happened. "Immediately her bleeding stopped" (Mark 5:29). Without a word, a look, or a touch from Jesus, she was made whole simply by believing He could heal her—and daring to act on that belief.

Higgs later writes that this woman "risked everything—public humiliation, if not punishment—to make her confession of faith." Her illness influenced her will (or desire) to believe and respond by reaching out and touching Jesus.

Often, when negative influences occur and human solutions become impossible, people become more inclined to seek the only One who can solve the problem. When the results of sin cause things like poverty, illness, and bondage, they engage the will negatively. In situations of despair, it is important not to allow our condition to limit our ability to align our will with God's will. It is this God-given tool of the will that gives us the power to align our will with God's and the ability to turn a bad situation into a beautiful and fulfilled purpose.

Thoughtful Moment

Scripture: Galatians 5:7–9 (ESV): "You were running well. Who hindered you from obeying the truth? This persuasion is not from him who calls you. A little leaven leavens the whole lump."

Conceptual Principle: The internal and external influences around us constantly affect the decisions of our will.

Question: Does the external and internal influence of your environment promote or reject God's will for your life?

Notes

Your Will Is Your Worship

Influence of the Will #26

Adoration is the spontaneous yearning of the heart to worship, honor, magnify, and bless God. We ask nothing but to cherish him. We seek nothing but his exaltation. We focus on nothing but his goodness.

—Richard J. Foster

Foundation Scripture: *John 4:24 (NLT): "For God is Spirit, so those who worship him must worship in spirit and in truth."*

I can often remember being willing to say "thank you" throughout the day to people I don't know or people whose names I have not even thought to ask. If someone opens the door for you, you are willing to say "thank you," or if someone allows you to pass by them, you thank that person. I have never seen someone be willing to stop to worship someone they do not know or have not had an encounter with. There are so many things for which we should be willing to say "thank You, God," and rightfully so, but to worship God is another level of reverence. Worship happens when God becomes so intimate with a person's life that it begins to serve His divine purpose and in return fulfills the person's destiny. Worshipping is a key factor in getting the Father's attention. When we convey reverence to our earthly fathers, it makes them smile because of our appreciation for what they have done. Our heavenly Father does the same when we take the time to thank Him through our worship and praise. He loves to be adored the way we love to be adored by someone we love.

I believe true success and life fulfillment is when the love God has given us through Christ Jesus begins to impact and cause restoration in others' lives. The apostle Paul said in his letter to the Ephesian church, "For we are his workmanship, created in Christ Jesus unto good works, which God hath before ordained that we should walk in them" (Ephesians 2:10 KJV). Being willing to worship requires you to have had an encounter or experience that was so impactful that it was one of a kind. Being willing to worship requires you to not think of yourself but of the goodness or kindness that has been shown to you. When we worship God, we are acknowledging the impact of His presence and being. It allows us to begin to see Him for all that He is in our lives. By seeing God, we can see our righteousness through Christ Jesus. Jesus Christ knew His affliction on the cross did not compare to the weight or value of glory that God would receive from the countless souls who would be saved because of His affliction. So when we become aware of God's spirit within us through Christ Jesus, we began to reflect the God likeness in our character and express glory through our lives. Similarly, Paul wrote, "For our light affliction, which is but for a moment, worketh for us a far more exceeding and eternal weight of glory" (2 Corinthians 4:17 KJV). This allows us to be thankful and appreciative of the righteousness He bestowed upon us. Because of His righteousness, we then begin to allow our lives to become overflowing with forgiveness and love for one another to the point that our lives become a vessel for God's glory. When we align our will with God's, we serve Him by serving others, which allows God's glory to be manifested in our lives. Thus, our service to Him is an expression of worship, acknowledging who God is.

Thoughtful Moment

Scripture: Isaiah 25:1 (NASB): "O Lord, You are my God; I will exalt You, I will give thanks to Your name; For You have worked wonders, Plans formed long ago, with perfect faithfulness."

Conceptual Principle: It is the nature of the human will, when properly cultivated, to give God glory and worship Him.

Question: How does God's goodness usher you to worship?

Notes

Our Words—An Expression of God's Will

INFLUENCE OF THE WILL #27

> With the tongue we praise our Lord and Father, and with it we curse human beings, who have been made in God's likeness. Out of the same mouth come praise and cursing. My brothers and sisters, this should not be.
>
> —James 3:9-10 (NIV)

Foundation Scripture: *Proverbs 10:6-11 (Benson Commentary): "The mouth of a righteous man is a well of life — Continually sending forth waters of life, or such words as are refreshing and useful, both to himself and others, both for the preserving of natural life, the promoting of spiritual, and ensuring of eternal life; As the mouth of a good man speaketh those things which are good and beneficial to himself and others, so the mouth of a wicked man uttereth violence, or injury, or things injurious to others, which at last fall upon himself."*

Due to the fact that believers have the mind of Christ and are created in God's image, our expressed thoughts have the potential to reveal God's will—His purposes. They also have the propensity to show human's fleshly thoughts. The writer of Proverbs wisely said, "Death and life are in the power of the tongue, and those who love it will eat its fruit" (Proverbs 18:21 NASB). The child of God's words can destroy or build up (Proverbs 12:16); they can express their will or God's will.

Thus, the believer's will is in their words, and when aligned with God's will, they have the incredible power to bring life, love, joy, and peace. However, the believer can also be filled with hate, deceit, and bitterness—everything contrary to God's perfect, holy nature.

What denotes whether a person's words will be filled with one or the other? The inner nature from which these words flow. Words are actually an overflow of what is stored in a person's heart. The writer of the gospel of Luke says, "The good person out of the good treasure of his heart produces good, and the evil person out of his evil treasure produces evil, for out of the abundance of the heart his mouth speaks" (Luke 6:45 ESV).

Once again, human beings are created in the image of God. Out of the overflow of God's heart, He speaks love, peace, patience, kindness, goodness, joy, faithfulness, and self-control. Everything that came into existence is an overflow of this fruit. What overflows from the believer's heart should stem from the same fruit of the Spirit—ultimately, from God's love. This, according to Colossians 1:9–12 (NIV), is God's will:

> For this reason, since the day we heard about you, we have not stopped praying for you and asking God to *fill you with the knowledge of his will* through all spiritual wisdom and understanding. And we pray this in order that you may live a life worthy of the Lord and may please him in every way, *bearing fruit in every good work*, growing in the knowledge of God, being strengthened with all power according to his glorious might so that you may have great endurance and patience, and joyfully giving thanks to the Father, who has qualified you to share in the inheritance of the saints in the kingdom of light. (emphasis added)

Thoughtful Moment

Scripture: Luke 6:45 (NASB): "The good man out of the good treasure of his heart brings forth what is good; and the evil man out of the evil treasure brings forth what is evil; for his mouth speaks from that which fills his heart."

Conceptual Principle: A human being's voice is their expressed thoughts coming into existence. Aligning our words with God's will allow God's glory to be expressed.

Question: How do your words express God's will on the earth?

Notes

Character's Influence on the Will

Influence of the Will #28

Character in a saint means the disposition of Jesus Christ persistently manifested.

—Oswald Chambers

Foundational Scripture: *1 Corinthians 10:31 (NIV): "So, whether you eat or drink, or whatever you do, do all to the glory of God."*

In a fast-paced world where we're trying to achieve success or celebrity status, we are missing out on one of the greatest gifts a person possesses. No matter how wealthy, how successful, or how powerful you are—or how much influence you think you have—character is the foundation to them all. Character is the mental and moral qualities distinctive to an individual. Character expresses how you think and what principles you believe in. Character is your natural moral position on the situations you face on a daily basis. This is why your character influences your will to either execute or refrain from initiating. Character also allows you to stand in opposition of something that clashed with your moral convictions. You can never willingly pursue something unless your character is in alignment with your will. The will constantly engages the character to determine the direction and destination for your life. Since Believers are the governmental influence and character of our king Jesus Christ, it is our responsibility to impact the world territories with His character, His will, His purpose, and His intent, which will produce a culture and moral character fit for a king and His children.

There is a familiar story about a man who saw a snake that was bruised and trying to get on the other side of a river. The man decided to help him by bandaging him up and putting him in his boat. He fed and nourished the snake along the journey. About midway to the shore, the snake started feeling better and crawled up close to the man and thanked him. The man told the snake he knew the snake was hurt and couldn't get cross the river alone, so he did what he thought was the right thing to do. So the snake and the man happily continued their journey across the river. They finally made it across the river to the edge, and the snake slithered out the boat on to the shore. Then the man got out the boat and started putting his things on the shore. When the man was done, he went near the snake to say goodbye. All of a sudden, the snake coiled back and bit the man. The man looked at the snake and asked why it had bitten him, and the snake said, "I am a snake—striking is in my character."

The moral of this story is that just as a snake's natural character is to bite, we are all designed with individual characters that serve our purposes. Humankind's natural character is to glorify God by doing good works. Just know that there are times when natural character conflicts, so we should all balance the will of our character to protect the future of our ability to maximize our purpose in life.

Thoughtful Moment

Scripture: Philippians 4:8 (ESV): "Finally, brothers, whatever is true, whatever is honorable, whatever is just, whatever is pure, whatever is lovely, whatever is commendable, if there is any excellence, if there is anything worthy of praise, think about these things."

Conceptual Principle: Character is constant, and the will to be in constant righteous character takes a willing heart. Character consists of the mental and moral qualities distinctive to an individual. Character is a spiritual component of human identity.

Question: How does your character influence your will?

Notes

The Will's Impact on Habits

INFLUENCE OF THE WILL #29

> The habit of always putting off an experience until you can afford it, or until the time is right, or until you know how to do it is one of the greatest burglars of joy. Be deliberate, but once you've made up your mind—jump in.
>
> —Chuck Swindoll

Foundational Scripture: *Philippians 4:13 (NKJV): "I can do all things through Christ who strengthens me."*

Habit is one of the analytical foundational tools for marketing. Companies are constantly monitoring your daily habits to determine how to market their products and services to you. This applies to every organization and marketplace you go to. It includes books that influence daily activities and situations. Your habits are the building blocks for the markets you live in. So if you are willing to change your routines, you can change what's being marketed to you on a daily basis.

Because habits are built on routines, they must engage your will. Have you ever created a routine you are not willing to pursue? This is why weight loss and negative addictions are so difficult. Habit helps you deal with what happens in life while the will engages the *whys* of life. There are so many things I started a routine for just to find out I was clueless about why I really started the routine. When I start analyzing the conditions of my will in a particular area in my life, I was able to sustain my habits by aligning my will to the purpose of my routines. It is like going to the swimming pool and never getting in the pool because you don't like to swim. At some point in the routine of your habit, you have to begin to be willing to pursue your purpose.

I remember at the age of ten waking up every morning at four o'clock during the summer to go chop cotton. We did this every morning until it was time to go on our summer vacation. My mother made it a routine to get out the house and get on that truck. I still remember hating to wake up to go get on that truck. It was like I was being punished for something I had no control over. Then we had to give our earnings to my mother, and maybe we got a few dollars to spend on what we wanted. I felt that way for about four weeks. Around that fifth week, I realized it was about time to go on vacation and I did not want to go without money. So the last few weeks turned from disappointment to excitement because I knew I was going have money to take on vacation. All of a sudden waking up early stopped being a problem. My routine finally found purpose, and I began to align my will with a purpose I was willing to pursue.

Thoughtful Moment

Scripture: Philippians 4:13 (KJV): "I can do all things through Christ Jesus which strengtheneth me."

Conceptual Principle: Habits are built on routine, but routine is the execution of an action. Actions are a byproduct of what you are willing to believe and do.

Question: What influences are creating your habits and routines that do not promote God's purpose for your life?

Notes

The Will to Take Control

INFLUENCE OF THE WILL #30

Let go of all your fears and worries and let God take over. Giving up control can be difficult but the changes you see in your life with be worth it.

—Lisa Rusczyk, EdD

Foundational Scripture: *Isaiah 55:8–9 (KJV): "For my thoughts are not your thoughts, neither are your ways my ways, saith the Lord. For as the heavens are higher than the earth, so are my ways higher than your ways, and my thoughts than your thoughts."*

There are times when life seems to be having its way with you. Sometimes it seems as if we are lost without help. Then there are times when we finally reach our wits' end and have to decide to trust God or continue living in a cycle of confusion. I have been in a few situations where I felt life wouldn't get any better until I decided to believe in God for something better. Being made in the image of God allows us to take control over our lives through His Word. God's Word supersedes our situation and causes change to happen for His glory. We only have to be willing to use God's Word in alignment with His will and purpose for our lives.

Rich Man and Ex-Beggar Story

> One day, a very wealthy man was walking on the road. Along the way, he saw a beggar on the sidewalk. The rich man looked kindly at the beggar and asked him why he was begging. The beggar said, "Sir, I've been unemployed for a year now. You look like a rich man. Sir, if you'll give me a job, I'll stop begging." The rich man smiled and said,

"I want to help you. But I won't give you a job. I'll do something better. I want you to be my business partner. Let's start a business together. The beggar blinked hard. He didn't understand what the older man was saying. "What do you mean, Sir? "I own a rice plantation. You could sell my rice in the market. I'll provide you the sacks of rice. I'll pay the rent for the market stall. All you'll have to do is sell my rice. And at the end of the month, as Business Partners, we'll share in the profits. Tears of joy rolled down his cheeks. "Oh Sir," he said, "you're a gift from Heaven. You're the answer to my prayers. Thank you, thank you, thank you!" He then paused and said, Sir, how will we divide the profits? Do I keep 10% and you get 90%? Do I keep 5% and you get 95%? I'll be happy with any arrangement. The rich man shook his head and chuckled. "No, I want you to give me the 2%. And you keep the 98%. For a moment, the beggar couldn't speak. He couldn't believe his ears. The deal was too good to be true. The rich man smiled. He said, "I don't need the money, my friend. I'm already wealthy beyond what you can ever imagine. I want you to give me 2% of your profits so you grow" The beggar knelt down before his benefactor and said, "Yes Sir, I will do as you say. I'm so grateful for what you're doing for me"! The beggar now dressed a little bit better, operated a store selling rice in the market. He worked very hard. He woke up early in the morning and slept late at night. And sales were brisk, also because the rice was of good quality. And after 30 days, the profits were astounding. At the end of the month, as the ex-beggar was counting the money, and liking the feeling of money in his hands, an idea grew in his mind. He told himself, Gee, why should I give 2% to my Business Partner? I didn't see him the whole month! I was the one who was working day and night for this business. I did all the work. I deserve 100% of the profits. The rich man came to collect his 2% of the profits. The ex-beggar

> said, "You don't deserve the 2%. I worked hard for this. I deserve all of it!" If you were his Business Partner, how would you feel? God is our business partner. God gave us life, every single breath. God gave us talents, ability to talk, to create, to earn money. God gave us a body, eyes, ears, mouth, hands, feet, a heart. God gave us a mind, body, imagination, emotions, reasoning, language. Don't forget to give back! (Akram, 2015)

Sometimes losing control of your life allows you to take control of your life. This is why God said in Matthew 16:25 (KJV): "For whosoever will save his life shall lose it: and whosoever will lose his life for my sake shall find it." Taking control can sometimes mean changing the geographical location of your life, but most of the time it has to do with aligning your thoughts with the direction you are aiming to go. I remember going to the doctor about having migraine headaches. My doctor asked the strangest question. He said, "Mr. Cotton, are you getting out and enjoying your life?" At first I got very offended because I thought his question was irrelevant to my migraines, but when I left his office that question stayed with me. So I began to start finding thing to do that I would enjoy. Later I realized that the migraines were fewer, and when I did get migraines, I could continue my day. I realized I had been giving my migraines too much control over my daily existence, and I could take that control back. Sometimes all it takes is a change in perspective about your situation in order to live a purposeful life. So regardless of your situation, you can still live a peaceful life once you know that your peace rests with the prince of peace, Jesus Christ. Life can only be lived successfully in Christ Jesus, not in wealth, power, or fame. These are only byproducts of the peace you have in Christ Jesus. So start today and tell that obstacle that's been promoting negative thoughts about you and the life God has for you to move so you can pursue the glorious life God has already predestined for you in Christ Jesus.

Thoughtful Moment

Scripture: 2 Timothy 1:7 (NKJV); Luke 10:19 (KJV): "For God has not given us a spirit of fear, but of power and of love and of a sound mind. Behold, I give unto you power to tread on serpents and scorpions, and over all the power of the enemy: and nothing shall by any means hurt you."

Conceptual Principle: God has placed humankind as the dominion authority on earth to express His will and create glory.

Question: What area of your life do you need to take dominion over using the authority Jesus Christ has given you?

Notes

CONCLUSION

Because our will is seated in our conscious and subconscious minds, we are constantly assessing the thoughts that engage our will. Our will is engaged through multiple levels of relationships, interactions, principles, reasons, intellect, and both internal and external influences. Every decision we make has an impact on and engages our will. Too often we are simply looking at the performance measurements of our will instead of the purpose and identity of the will. This allows us only to assess the symptoms of the will executed, not the purpose and conditioning of the will. We are creatures of habit by nature, but habits are based on routines of actions, not on understanding or truth. This is why we can go to church, school, and the marketplace routinely without a true sense of a willing purpose. This generally leaves us empty of purpose and eventually exhausted from failed attempts.

This why Jesus Christ paid the redemptive price for our sins and brought us access back into proper relationship with God our father: "And he is the propitiation for our sins: and not for ours only, but also for the sins of the whole world" (1 John 2:2 KJV). "In this was manifested the love of God toward us, because that God sent his only begotten Son into the world, that we might live through him. Herein is love, not that we loved God, but that he loved us, and sent his Son to be the propitiation for our sins" (1 John 4:9-10 KJV). You are first self-sustainable with God alone and then someone who is also self-sustainable with God alone comes and connects their God-given talent to produce maximum glory for God in the relationship. We are who we are created to be—God's children. We are made in His image and likeness for the purpose of bringing God's heavenly culture to earth. It takes the revelation of God's Word to penetrate our hearts and minds so that our will is engaged to be aligned with God's will. This book is meant to begin the dialog between your will and the influences it engages on a daily basis. I believe that once we begin to view our will in alignment with God's will because of our God-given identity, we can overcome the challenges of internal and external influences that try to persuade our purpose toward negative and useless meaning.

A CALL TO SALVATION AND REGENERATION ACTION PLAN

Salvation and Regeneration

Often Christians draw their theology from hymns and worship songs. We sing, "Earth and heaven will bow in awe, joining in salvation's song,"(Townend & Small, 2007) and "My God is mighty to save," (Fielding & Morgan, 2006) which are beautiful confessions of faith, but we don't *really* understand what the term *salvation* means. We bundle the term together with other theological terms when they—though they might be similar—have different meanings.

Salvation

The term *salvation* means "the process of being transformed after experiencing rebirth in Christ Jesus." It is not a one-time event that happens and then is complete; salvation is ongoing. Paul told the Philippians to "*continue* to work out your salvation" (Philippians 2:12 NIV, emphasis added)—indicating that salvation is ongoing. Thus, when Paul called believers not to be conformed to the world but "be transformed by the renewing of your mind, so that you may prove what the will of God is" (Romans 12:2 NASB), he meant to be changing continually in character. When a person receives Jesus, they receive the Holy Spirit, who begins the conviction and growth process of the heart and mind.

Paul said in Romans 12:2 that when a person's mind is renewed, he or she can then "prove" what the good, acceptable, and perfect will of God is. Understanding what happens when a person believes in Jesus—the perfect substitute offering who provided justification for sin and allowed His people to be presented holy before Him—is paramount. It is a call to salvation, but it is also a call to be justified, sanctified, and ultimately regenerated. It is a call to be brought near the One who is in the business of restoration and to be transformed on the journey.

Is God calling you?

Jesus Christ, Justification for the World

Justification is a legal term commonly used in a courtroom setting. In any court setting, a judge always determines the justice of the case. In humanity's case of justice, the courtroom featured Satan as the plaintiff, humanity as the defendant, Jesus Christ as the evidence, and God as the judge. Satan, the accuser, stated all the evidence of humanity's past and its imperfect attempts in the future.

One of Satan's main pieces of evidence was Adam's and Eve's fall in the Garden of Eden. Because Adam and Eve started mankind, Satan assumed that every man born from them would receive their sinful nature. He knew that every other mankind would have to come from them and therefore would not be able to replace the original relationship between man and God, by being born in sin, leaving humanity forever trapped in sin and unable to be back in their proper relationship with God.

At first, the case for humanity appeared hopeless—that is, until Jesus Christ entered the courtroom and began to testify. Scripture declares that we overcome the devil by the word of our testimony (Revelation 12:11). Jesus Christ first stated He was born of the Holy Spirit on the earth, just as Adam was born from the Father. This birth validated His presence as a witness for humanity's case.

Then Jesus began to state how sin entered humanity through the rebellion of one man: Adam. Sin became part of humankind's nature because all human beings after Adam came from his genetic coding. Through Jesus's sacrifice, however, the penalty for sin was paid in full.

Because the man Jesus Christ died on the cross, humanity's sin nature passed through Adam, and all sin of rebellion is now able to be justified in Jesus Christ's death, burial, and resurrection. Humanity, therefore, is justified from Satan's accusation, his case of sin, and any condemnation. Now, all men and women can be reborn in Jesus Christ by accepting Him as their Lord and Savior and receiving the Holy Spirit as a comfort and guide.

Jesus Christ, Sanctification for All

Believing in what Jesus's death did begin the process of sanctification. The word *sanctified* means we have been made holy or set apart for God's use. The Bible provides several illustrations of events and articles that were set apart only for God's use. God's feasts in Leviticus 23, for example, were declared holy. Items in the temple were also sanctified for God's use, with the blood of the sacrifices sprinkled on them for the atonement of the people's sin.

Not only did the blood of Jesus Christ atone for the sin of humanity, it also removed the sin and condemnation penalty. Choosing to sin and rebelling against God involves refusing to allow our will to be aligned with God's plans for our lives.

Paul said, however, that people are made holy too: "For both he that sanctifieth and they who are sanctified are all of one: for which cause he is not ashamed to call them brethren" (Hebrews 2:11 KJV). This can only happen when a person puts their faith in Christ—because human beings cannot sanctify themselves. Only God can declare a person holy. It is "because of him that you are in Christ Jesus, who has become for us wisdom from God—that is, our righteousness, holiness and redemption" (1 Corinthians 1:30 NIV). Thus, followers of Christ are sanctified, set apart for God's use:

> Such were some of you. But you were washed, but you were sanctified, but you were justified in the name of the Lord Jesus and by the Spirit of our God. (1 Corinthians 6:11 NKJV)

God is holy, and anything that comes into His presence must also be holy. Without Christ, human beings simply cannot be in God's presence. Jesus sanctifies and places those who believe in Him in right alignment and relation with God.

Regeneration: Accepting Jesus Christ as Lord and Savior

Once a person is sanctified, the process of regeneration begins—accepting one's original genetic essence. This is what it means to be reborn.

Every person comes from and is created by God through Adam but also retains a sin nature because of Adam. Rebirth is the process of being born again, as distinguished from one's first birth, which without Christ leaves a person "dead in [their] transgressions and sins" (Ephesians 2:1 NIV).

The word *regeneration* is only found in Matthew 19:28 and Titus 3:5. This word, *paliggenesia* in ancient Greek, means a "new birth." (BibleHub, n.d.) In Matthew 19:28 this word is equivalent to the "restitution of all things" (Acts 3:21). In Titus 3:5, it indicates a change of heart that other New Testament scriptures describe as passing from death to life (1 John 3:14), becoming a new creature in Christ Jesus (2 Corinthians 5:17), being born again (John 3:5), renewal of the mind (Romans 12:2), resurrection from the dead (Ephesians 2:6), or being quickened (Ephesians 2:1, 5).

This change is ascribed to the Holy Spirit. It does not originate with humankind, but with God (John 1:12–13, 2:29, 5:11). For God is holy, and everything connected to Him must also be holy.

When a person accepts rebirth and regeneration in Christ, he or she is radically changed. The person's soul's disposition is made new, or sanctified—made holy—and he or she is accepted into fellowship with the Father. His regeneration bridges the great chasm that sin creates and prevents a person from experiencing intimacy with God.

God's process of regeneration brings the person back into a close relationship with Him. Regeneration is what God does at the moment of salvation.

Because of this mystery of regeneration, Paul could proclaim:

> And be not conformed to this world: but be ye transformed by the renewing of your mind that ye may prove what [is] that good, and acceptable, and perfect, will of God. (Romans 12:2 KJV)

When we accepted Jesus, we were saved, justified, made holy, and regenerated for something that goes far beyond personal fulfillment—although Jesus provides complete joy and satisfaction to all who believe. We were saved, justified, sanctified, and regenerated for a greater purpose: to publish to the world God's "good, and acceptable, and perfect" will (Cotton, 2018).

ROMAN ROAD TO SALVATION

The Roman Road is a pathway you can walk. It is a group of Bible verses from the book of Romans in the New Testament. If you walk down this road, you will end up understanding how to be saved.

Admit That You Are a Sinner.
Romans 3:10: As it is written. There is none righteous, no not one.
Romans 3:23: For all have sinned, and come short of the glory of God.
Romans 5:12: Wherefore, as by one man sin entered into the world, and death by sin; and so death passed upon all men, for that all have sinned.

Sin Has an Ending ... It Results in Death.
Romans 6:23a: For the wages of sin is death ... We all owe this wage of spiritual death described in Revelation 20:14: You need to be born again!

Realize That God Loves You!
Romans 5:8: But God commendeth his love toward us, in that, while we were yet sinners, Christ died for us. When Jesus died on the cross He paid sin's penalty.

Salvation Is a Free Gift from God to You!
Romans 6:23b, ... but the gift of God is eternal life through Jesus Christ our Lord. You can't earn this gift, but you must reach out and receive it.

You Must Ask God to Forgive You and Save You.
Romans 10:9-10, That if thou shall confess with thy mouth the Lord Jesus, and shalt believe in thine heart that God hath raised him from the dead, thou shall be saved. For with the heart man believeth unto righteousness; and with the mouth confession is made unto salvation.

Like Any Gift It Must Be Received!
Romans 10:13: For whosoever shall call upon the name of the Lord shall be saved. (Bruce, 1995)

REFERENCES

Akram, Shadab. 2015. "What's A Good Short Story with A Moral About Responsibility/Roles In A Community?" https://www.quora.com/Whats-a-good-short-story-with-a-moral-about-responsibility-roles-in-a-community.

Bridges, Jerry. "25 Jerry Bridges Christian Quotes". Accessed December 6, 2018. https://www.christianquotes.info/quotes-by-author/jerry-bridges-quotes.

Brown, Dan. "God's Will is Your Deepest Desires." Accessed December 6, 2018. https://www.goodreads.com/quotes/351899-god-s-will-is-your-deepest-desires.

Bruce, Aaron. 1995. "Roman Road To Salvation." www.lightinside.org/light/Romans/Rod/20Teaching.

Chambers, Oswald. 2018. "The Place of Exaltation." https://utmost.org/the-place-of-exaltation.

Cotton, Hermon T. 2018. *Our Will Is God's Will: Using Our Will to Pursue God's Will For A Glorious Life.* Kentucky: Sermon to Sermon.

Dungy, Tony. 2007. "Quiet Strength: A Memoir – The Principles, Practices, and Priorities of A Winning." https://www.pinterest.com/pin/97249673178491928/

Faust, James. "James E. Faust Quotes." Accessed December 6, 2018. https://www.brainyquote.com/quotes/james_e_faust_621216.

Fielding, Ben and Reuben Morgan. 2006. "Mighty to Save." Hillsong United.

Foster, Richard J. 2001. "Adoration is the Spontaneous Yearning of the Heart to Worship Honor." https://quotefancy.com/quote/1523213/Richard-J-Foster-Adoration-is-the-spontaneous-yearning-of-the-heart-to-worship-honor.

Guaderruma, Ivan. "Christian Quotes." Accessed December 6, 2018. https://www.pinterest.com/pin/547398529692923764.

Higgs, Liz Curtis. 2017. "The Woman Who Touched Jesus." https://www.todayschristianwoman.com/articles/2007/january/woman-who-touched-jesus.html

Ironside, Harry. 2018. "Full Assurance." https://www.raptureready.com/full-assurance-harry-ironside.

Johnson, Dani. 2009. "Spirit-Driven Success Learn Time Tested Biblical Secrets to Create Wealth While Serving Others." https://www.wow4u.com/decisions-quotes/.

Lewis, C.S. "God Knows Our Situation He Will Not Judge Us As." Accessed December 6, 2018. https://www.goodreads.com/quotes/8553751-god-knows-our-situation-he-will-not-judge-us-as.

Lucado, Max. 2015. "Just Like Jesus." https://maxlucado.com/products/just-like-jesus.

Moody, Dwight, L. "Moody Sermons." Accessed December 6, 2018. https://www.biblebelievers.com/moody_sermons/m22.html.

Munroe, Myles. 2018. *The Principles and Power of Kingdom Citizenship.* Shippensburg: Destiny Image Publishers, Inc.

Murdock, Mike. "7 Laws of Uncommon Success." Accessed December 6, 20118. https://www.pinterest.com/pin/19703317091258572/

Nduwe, Kalu. "Kalu Ndukwe Kalu Quotes." Accessed December 6, 2018. https://www.goodreads.com/author/quotes/2895377.Kalu_Ndukwe_Kalu.

Nee, Watchman. 1993. "Watchman Nee Quotes." https://www.christianquotes.info/quotes-by-author/watchman-nee- quotes.

Osteen, Joel. "Joel Osteen Quotes." Access December 6, 2018. https://www.wow4u.com/opportunity.

Rodgers, Adrian. 2013. "22 Encouraging Adrian Rodgers Quotes." https://www.whatchristianswanttoknow.com/22-encouraging-adrian-rodgers-quotes.

Roosevelt, Eleanor. "Inspiring Quotes Eleanor Roosevelt." Accessed December 6, 2018. https://inspiration.allwomenstalk.com/inspiring-quotes-from-eleanor-roosevelt.

Rusczyk, Lisa. "50 Things to Know About Prayer: Practical Prayer Tips from a Mom." Accessed December 6, 2018. https://www.wow4u.com/letting-go-quotes/

Salk, Jonas. "Jonas Salk Qutoes." Accessed December 6, 2018. https://www.brainyquote.com/quotes/jonas_salk_389658.

Spurgeon, Charles. 2015. "Every Christian Has A Choice Between Being Humble." https://gracequotes.org/quote/every-christian-has-a-choice-between-being-humble.

St. Bernard of Clairveux. "God Will Become Visible As Gods Image Is Reborn In You." Accessed December 6, 2018. https://quotefancy.com/quote/1545672/Bernard-of-Clairvaux-God-will-become-visible-as-God-s-image-is-reborn-in-you.

Swindoll, Chuck. "Chuck Swindoll." Accessed December 6, 2018. https://www.christianquotes.info/quotes-by-author/chuck-swindoll-quotes.

Townend, Stuart and Andrew Small. 2007. "Salvation's Song." Thankyou Music (adm. By CapitolCMG Publishing.com, Integrity Music).

Warren, Rick. "12 Inspiration Rick Warren Quotes on Forgiveness." Accessed December 6, 2018. ipost.christianpost.com/post/12-inspirational-rick-warren-quotes-on-forgiveness.

Wigglesworth, Smith. 2015. "Gifts of Healing and Miracles." www.smithwigglesworth.com/sermons/eif15.htm.

"3824. paliggenesia." From Strong's Concordance. Bible Hub. http://biblehub.com/greek/3824.htm.

ABOUT THE AUTHOR

Hermon T. Cotton is a veteran with twenty-plus years of service, a published author, and an inspirational speaker who addresses critical issues impacting individuals' will in the area of social, organizational, and spiritual development. He has addressed and ministered on multiple platforms concerning spiritual development throughout his more than fifteen years following Jesus Christ. Since the will is one of the vital components of the soul, it is paramount that we discover God's purpose for the will. In 2005 he became very intrigued with understanding whether free will was really free and whether there was any way of understanding how to walk in God's will in our lives. He realized he was being influenced by the world's advertisement and marketing strategies. At other times he was simply managing life according to his own will. So he began to seek God for His understanding of the will, since He created it. Since that time Hermon's life has never been the same. Hermon's prayer is that you gain control over the influences of your will so that God can get maximum glory out of your life.

Hermon is also the author of "OUR WILL IS GOD'S WILL". You can get a copy at Amazon and AuthorHouse.

Printed in the United States
By Bookmasters